Singlehanding

A Sailor's Guide

Tony Meisel

Stanley Paul
London Melbourne Auckland Johannesburg

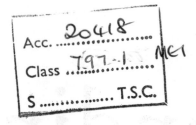
Stanley Paul & Co. Ltd

An imprint of Century Hutchinson Ltd
Brookmount House, 62-65 Chandos Place,
Covent Garden, London WC2N 4NW

Century Hutchinson Australia (Pty) Ltd
PO Box 496, 16-22 Church Street, Hawthorn,
Melbourne, Victoria 3122

Century Hutchinson, New Zealand Limited
32-34 View Road, PO Box 40-086, Glenfield,
Auckland 10

Century Hutchinson South Africa (Pty) Ltd
PO Box 337, Bergvlei 2012, South Africa

First published in 1987

British Library Cataloguing in Publication Data

Meisel, Tony
  Singlehanding: a sailor's guide
  1. Sailing, Single-handed
  I. Title
  623.88'223   GV811

ISBN 0 09 172 650 6

This book was designed and produced by
Footnote Productions Ltd
The Old Brewery
6 Blundell Street
London N7 9BH

Editorial Director: Sheila Rosenzweig Buff
Art Director: Judith Ann Doud

Manufactured in Hong Kong by Regent Publishing
Services Ltd
Printed by Leefung-Asco Printers Limited, Hong
Kong

Contents

Introduction:
Alone at the Helm

Everyone singlehands. Usually you just don't realize you're doing it. When you go out for a day's sail or a cruise to a nearby port, you probably raise sail, leave the mooring, make passage, navigate and arrive with little or no help. Sure, you may have crew, and you may depend on them now and then, but the essential operation of the vessel is in your hands.

Singlehanding: A Sailor's Guide gives you hard information, based on my own experience and that of many other singlehanders, on how to better manage and operate your boat without the reluctant aid of others. This is not a book for would-be Slocums or Chichesters, though the information still applies. Rather, it is for the average sailor of reasonable accomplishment who wishes to cruise along the coast, with an occasional foray offshore.

It will show you how to use your present skills to make safe, swift passages solo—and how to add to your storehouse of knowledge and techniques, to do alone what you have traditionally thought you needed others to help with. You'll learn how to economically modify your deck layout and rig to make your boat a safe, easily managed platform. You'll learn to plan ahead and think out all your maneuvers—along with alternatives— for every possible contingency. You'll learn to ship out day and night with confidence.

This manual will help sharpen techniques for changing headsails, rigging self-steering, reefing, anchoring, mooring and docking, and maintaining your boat by yourself. You will even come to feel comfortable about docking under sail—with practice. Most important, you will gain confidence in your abilities and in yourself.

Obviously, all of this demands time and practice, and there are no guarantees at sea. But you will slowly begin to understand the lure of solo sailing—the pleasure of a warm evening at the helm, the knowledge and satisfaction that you've made a safe and successful landfall, and no one has done it but you, your hands, your brain, your instincts. In a crowded, inflationary, mechanically inept world, that is satisfaction indeed. To weather a storm at sea and make port is one of the great thrills of a lifetime. You earn the kind of self-esteem that is very rare today.

Furthermore, even with others along for the ride, you will, through your experience, know what to do, no matter what. And there may be times when you are the only one who can bring the ship home safely. This book won't take you to hell and back, but it may help you avoid hell altogether.

Tony Meisel
New Suffolk, New York

1. Boat Types and Rigs

If you already have a boat, and intend to keep it, read the next chapter. If you're in the market, and plan to do a lot of sailing alone, keep reading . . .

The first question asked by any prospective buyer is invariably, "How big?" The second is, "How many does she sleep?" Both are perfectly reasonable questions if you have a large family or if you suffer delusions of grandeur. However, as a potential singlehander you really need only two berths, one to port, one to starboard.

Size is another matter. Since a boat's speed (we are speaking of displacement monohulls, not multihulls and such) is directly proportional to its waterline length (1.34 times the square root of that dimension in feet), you must decide how quickly you wish to move. Of course, this is not the only criterion, but it is a good assumption with which to estimate speed. Assuming similar rig configurations, sail area to displacement ratios, and hull shapes, a yacht with a LWL of 30 feet (9 meters) will easily pass anything with a LWL of 24 feet (7.2 meters).

But in assessing the size boat you want, speed cannot be the only consideration. Actually, the first question to ask is, "How much can I afford?" Boats, like cheese, are sold more or less by weight. A light displacement yacht will usually cost less than a moderate or heavy one of the same length. The argument over displacement rages on and is not entirely rational, despite the figures and equations thrown about. True, light displacement needs less sail area, smaller sails, lighter rigging, smaller fittings, less engine power, etc. To offset these advantages, consider also: more lively motion in a seaway, smaller tank capacity, less storage space, no bilges to speak of and fewer creature comforts. If you want refrigeration, generators, 200 gallons (900 litres) of water, massive instrumentation, hot water heaters and reverse osmosis watermakers, your light displacement boat will have changed dramatically to a moderate to heavy boat, sail far below its designed lines and no longer have any of the advantages you originally bought it for.

On the other hand, though a heavy displacement vessel will hold everything, it will demand far greater sail area, sail less than spectacularly in heavier weather and eat a large hole in your wallet. It will be more comfortable, have a gentler motion in a seaway, but at a price of greater effort to sail.

Like all good things in life, moderation usually holds our esteem and love the longest. It is not the passion of the light and racy, it isn't the security and sybaritic comfort of the heavy, but it can be a combination—if you get the compromises right—of the two. The days when each and every boat was a one-off creation of a master craftsman have passed, unless you can afford to indulge any whimsy, and few of us can take the time to build our own in the backyard. To find the perfect boat for you will take a long and hard and, I fear, dispassionate search.

Considering that after your house, a yacht is the most expensive object you will own, do try to be level-headed about its purchase. Too often, the process becomes a parody of falling over the deep end in love, and the results are equally disastrous. A moderate displacement yacht will last in your affections in the same way the partners in a marriage discover the good and lasting aspects of their relationship. Of course, you must make your own mistakes. I have been through four boats in my adult life, ranging from 45 feet (13.5 metres) down to 15 feet (5.5 metres), and the largest was by no means the best for me. No doubt, you will have to make your own mistakes. My argument for moderation is an attempt to help you avoid some of the costly possible errors.

A moderate boat—moderate in all respects—will not offer the spellbinding speed of light displacement, nor the room of a Colin Archer, but it will sail better, handle better and offer a good compromise between comfort and despair. The definitions of light, moderate and heavy have changed over the past decades, mostly as a result of promotional efforts on the part of boat-builders. I am not going to go into a technical discussion of what constitutes what, but a length/displacement ratio of 200 to 300 seems to be the best guideline. In actual terms, a 30-footer (9 meters) weighing between 8,500 and 10,000 pounds (3,900 and 4,500 kilos) can be considered moderate depending on beam, length waterline and the ratio of hull weight to ballast and fittings.

Now, the majority of boats built today are designed to give you the greatest volume for the money, a marketing ploy based on the fact that most people buy without sailing first and that the interior appointments sell a yacht. If you are singlehanding, the interior is important, but not for these reasons. What matters most is that the boat should be easy to sail, have a fair degree of directional stability and be comfortable for the purposes you have in mind. What is a pleasure for weekending will most likely not work if you are planning to cross oceans. Requirements dictate shape, size and capabilities.

If we were to construct an "ideal" 30-footer (9 meters) for the would-be singlehander it might have the following dimensions:

LOA 30 ft. (9 meters)
LWL 26 ft. (8 meters)
Beam 9 ft. (3 meters)
Draft 4.5 ft. (1.4 meters)
SA (working) 450 sq. ft. (40.5 sq. meters)
Displacement 9000 lbs. (4050 kilos)
Ballast 4000 lbs. (1800 kilos)

Our hypothetical yacht is designed with the following criteria in mind:

1. Ease of handling: a cutter rig, outboard rudder, clear decks, protected cockpit
2. Directional stability: moderately long keel, large rudder mounted on skeg, balanced sail plan
3. Speed: low wetted surface, canoe body with balanced ends, powerful sail plan
4. Comfort: good bunks, easy-to-use galley, low ballast, hull form of minimum pitching and gentle motion at sea
5. Simplicity: a real "killer" since part of the fun of owning a yacht is to be able to add goodies. But the sad fact is that anything mechanical or electrical will eventually break down when attacked by moisture and salt. There are *no* exceptions! Constant maintenance may be fun to some, but I would rather spend my time sailing. Few winches, few electrics, few instruments and as little in the way of gadgets as possible will make sailing a sport and a pasttime, not a gruelling maintenance schedule. More on this later.

I do not mean to imply that a 30-foot (9 meters) boat is right for you. Your combination of needs and desires may well dictate another size. But keep in mind your use patterns and your skills. While a very experienced sailor may well be able to handle a 45-foot (13.5 meters) ketch solo, another may feel more comfortable and may actually sail a 35-foot (10.5 meters) yacht better and faster. Having singlehanded a 21-foot (6.3 meters) sloop to Bermuda and back (from Long Island) I know it can be done, but I have absolutely no desire to ever repeat the effort and discomfort involved.

The 30-foot (9 meters) cutter was chosen because it is small enough to be sailed by one, comfortable enough for a couple and can take another couple as occasional guests. At the same time, it will hold the stores and tankage sufficient for an extended voyage solo. The sails will be of easily manageable size, maintenance can be kept to a minimum, and you will be able to enjoy the sailing, not the effort.

Whatever boat you choose, do be sure it can accommodate the tasks you wish it to. You won't be singlehanding all the time, after all. You will need accommodations and stowage for potential crew. You will probably need a working head and a galley to cope with guests and more guests. Just another set of criteria to work into that ever-compromising equation.

What I'm about to discuss has been covered by hundreds of experienced sailors, builders and designers before, and probably better, but for what it's worth I'm going to throw my opinion in. Sloops, cutters, ketches, yawls, catboats, schooners—these are the basic rig types. They can be mounted on assorted hulls, with different keel and rudder configurations, and they all work with a greater or lesser degree of efficiency. What we're concerned with here is rig *efficiency* balanced against *ease of handling*. After all you won't have a brace of hands for each sheet and halyard.

Single sticks have a host of advantages: simplicity, versatility, minimum windage, windward efficiency and less expense, and the

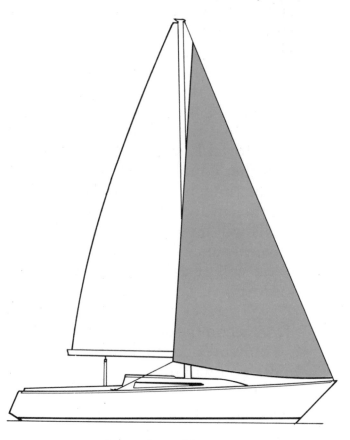

The sloop is certainly the simplest modern rig. Contemporary versions tend to have large foretriangles at the expense of the main.

thought of losing a mast and being left with nothing can be softened somewhat by jury rig planning. But that's not our concern here.

Most offshore sailors have come to appreciate the advantages of the cutter, its sail combinations and the ability to easily and quickly balance the sails for varying conditions. Even crusty Eric Hiscock has finally come around. Up to about 50 feet (15 meters) LOA, there is probably no competition. Even on small boats, twin headsails can smooth things out. Witness

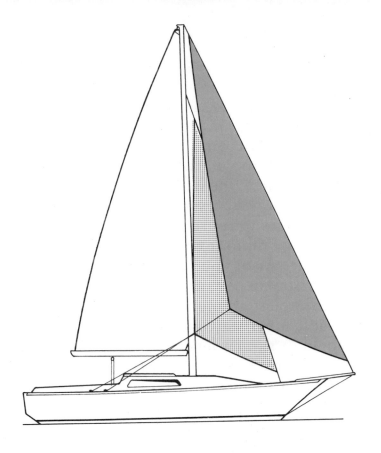

Cutter-rigged yachts have much of the simplicity of a sloop but with the added advantage that breaking up the foretriangle makes for easier handling, especially as the sail area increases. Additionally, better balance can be achieved, with more possible sail combinations.

John Letcher's *Aleutka* and Chuck Paine's *Frances* class. Though the sloop is a little less complicated, it is not nearly so versatile.

One of the proponent cries of "cutter folk" is the self-tacking staysail. Having undertaken a few long passages with this rig, I am not totally happy with it. Club booms are potentially dangerous and add to deck

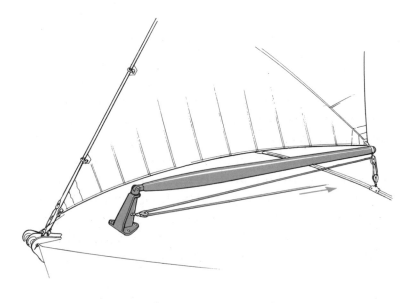

A club boom on the foredeck can be a hazard underway, though it will make for easier handling and fewer winches in the cockpit.

clutter. Furthermore, an overlapping staysail, loose footed, is far more efficient. Club sails are useless off the wind, less than overwhelming to windward and okay on a reach. Of course, the lack of boom means another set of winches and more sheets, but the advantages for pure sailing enjoyment outweigh the minor extra work, to my way of thinking. Also, you can set other sails from the inner stay in certain conditions.

The simplest arrangement is to have a removable inner stay, attached to the deck by a Hyfield or similar lever. The stay is braced, not by runners but by shrouds running aft from the mast tangs to just abaft the inner aft shrouds. This gives permanent strength without the bother of jumper struts or running backstays. The inner stay should be reasonably well separated from the forestay— by at least 2 or 3 feet (60 or 90 cm)—for easy tacking of the jib or yankee.

You will need two sets of leads, both port and starboard, of course. Try to get the yankee cut lower than usual, to keep the sheet from running so far aft that turning blocks are needed. A slightly larger yankee can be arranged for reefing, cutting out the need for an intermediate genny. I don't like turning blocks; they increase chafe, put enormous strains on the deck, and one once exploded on me. Not a pretty sight!

Simplest of all are catboats, but their suitability for passage-making is severely hampered by their inherent lack of balance and poor windward ability. Two-masted rigs of any sort add mechanical complication, expense, windage and diminished ability to point. That leaves us with sloops and cutters. A cutter is not a sloop with an inner forestay!

The center of effort of each is radically different because of mast position and the

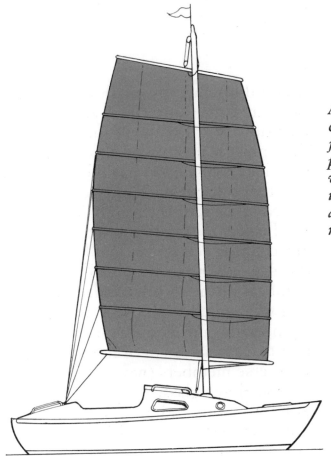

Another alternative for the cruising singlehander is the junk rig. Though not particularly strong to windward, it is the ultimate in quick reefing and below-decks manipulation.

increased sail area in the fore triangle of the cutter. A cutter under main alone will probably have greater lee helm than a sloop under the same sail. However, the textbook dictum about handling under main alone can be modified these days. Foresails are so efficient and easily handled that, for safety if nothing else, how a boat behaves under jib or staysail is probably as, if not, more important. Besides which, mains have shrunk to less than 50 percent of total working area on most boats.

The staying of a cutter rig, or any rig for that matter, is of paramount importance. Rig strength is determined by spar section, compression strength and resistance to mast bend. That is, ideally the stick should stay upright and straight while the rigging and heel of the mast absorb the stresses and loads.

In keeping a mast in a boat, the standing rigging acts as a web support. It allows the fore-and-aft and athwartships alignment of the spar. Unfortunately, it also pushes the mast downward with enormous force. This force must somehow be absorbed. The most effective arrangement has the mast stepped directly on the keel. This does *not* mean butted up against the lead ballast.

The keel in traditional wooden construction served (and still does, of course) as the backbone to which all the structural members of the ship were tied. The ballast in turn was bolted to the keel. In a properly engineered—and few are—modern fiberglass boat there is a system of longitudinal and transverse members (wood, foam, hollow glass sections) glassed into the boat along with bulkheads and deck to form a monocoque structure. These internal stiffeners serve the same functions as did keels, ribs, clamps and shelves of yore. In too many boats today there is little evidence of reinforcing structural members, and hence less than optimal strength for offshore work.

A classic case is Webb Chiles's experience, related in his book *Storm Passage*. His stock 37-foot (11 meters) cutter was without stringers or a floor pan. In his round-the-world voyage, the compression of the mast in heavy weather caused a rupture of the keel and massive leaking, almost causing him to founder.

If you are taking a boat offshore, you can be sure that the forces the mast and rigging will place upon the structure of the boat will be severe. That compressive force must be effectively absorbed without sacrificing smartness under a press of sail, or the watertight integrity of the hull. Provided the keel is structurally part of the boat, it can best absorb those strains. Therefore, a keel-stepped mast, or one thrusting upon a web floor system, is best. Deck-stepped masts are convenient, cheaper and, consequently, more widely used, and allow for a more weathertight deck. However, the deck must be carefully reinforced at the heel of the mast, and there must be a substantial bulkhead directly underneath or a mast compression pillar in the same location. Still, you sacrifice ultimate strength.

Standing rigging deserves equal consideration. The practice of a few years ago—forestay, backstay, uppers, double lowers—is hard to beat. With a cutter, add an inner forestay with either runners, jumpers or additional aft lowers.

Modern racing practice has had its influence, and not all to the good. However, the super-rigs of Tim Stearns or Ridder and Bergstrom don't concern us here. Hydraulics, triple spreaders, bendy masts and such have no place on a cruising boat. We're after simplicity.

Swept-back spreaders, babystays and fractional rigs are less demanding in terms of compression but have certain disadvantages for cruising. They cause chafe, and if one stay goes, the whole rig will probably topple over the side. Remember, you are alone. There's no one else to twang strings and fiddle with backstay adjusters. Nothing, for the committed cruising man, beats a masthead rig for strength and simplicity.

Assuming you accept this solution, certain procedures should be followed to ensure rig integrity. First and foremost, chainplates must be properly anchored and aligned. Once again, the pulling forces put upon them are very great, and they have to be through-bolted to a structural member and glassed in. They must also be of heavy enough section, long enough to distribute the forces, and of reasonable tensile strength to accommodate the bending and twisting—inadvertent or not—that they are subject to. More and more, chainplates are set inboard, which certainly enhances windward performance and, with today's beamy boats, allows spreaders of less than 6 feet (1.8 meters). But it is harder to securely attach them to cabin sides or decks. You often see glass fractures where the plates enter the deck, a sign of probable later trouble.

Having established our anchoring points, and assuming that wire rope will go between the masthead and those points, it might be a good idea to take the time to consider the devices used to attach and adjust the rigging. Long gone are the days of deadeyes and lanyards, wire loops and strap tangs. Now we've got Norseman and Sta-Lock terminals,

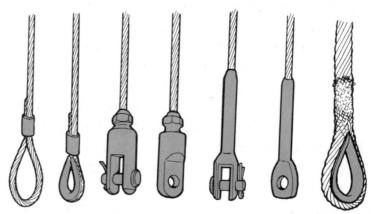

Possible eye- and fork-end fittings. From left: Talurit or Nicopress fitting; the same with thimble; Sta-Lok fork; Sta-Lok eye; swaged fork; swaged eye; splice with thimble. For the singlehander, end fittings installable on board, such as Sta-Lok or Norseman terminals, are preferred.

swaging, turnbuckles, T-ball terminals and rod rigging.

Swaging is the norm for attaching end fittings to wire, and it works quite well. For offshore purposes it has one disadvantage. Unless you have a swaging machine or replacement rigging aboard, you can't replace rigging. Sta-Lock and Norseman fittings, and others of the same ilk, such as Castlock epoxy fittings (though I've personally had no experience with these), seem to provide a comparatively simple solution to do-it-yourself rigging, especially in times of rising labor costs. They have been tested to equal the strength of the wire and can be installed with a few simple tools, if you follow instructions carefully.

T-ball terminals are eminently convenient for racing classes and trailer-sailers, but I have seen one rip through a mast wall on one occasion and would prefer not to have them aboard a cruising boat. Rod rigging has no place on a singlehander's boat. It can't be repaired, and you can't very well carry a spare rod. It's expensive and subject to sudden failure, unlike wire, which can be inspected regularly.

Through-bolted tangs smartly pinned with cotters and bolted-on spreaders seem to be the best solution for the cruising sailor. Most spreader ends are terribly designed. There really ought to be a captive device, smooth and rounded, to hold the uppers in position and lessen the need for windage-producing chafe pads.

Currently in fashion are stainless steel turnbuckles. Fine, except for two small items. One, stainless steel is subject—no matter what the grade—to sudden failure from oscillation fatigue, and you can't know beforehand when it will go. Second, stainless turnbuckle threads can gall and bind unless they are the rolled and not the standard cut threads. Hasselfors of Sweden is the only rolled thread rigging screw I know of.

One of the so-called silicon bronzes is probably most reliable for turnbuckle manufacture. Several different bronzes exist and you'd have to be a metallurgist to distinguish between them. The rigging screw market is dominated by an aluminum-silicon-nickel-copper mixture, which works just fine.

I must admit to a prejudice in favor of good, old fashioned fork-and-fork screws because, if your swaged fitting goes, you can more easily rig in a jury fitting. The most ingenious design, and one that is suitable, at the moment, only for small boats, is made by Johnson Marine in Connecticut. Based on an L. Francis Herreshoff prototype, it is the essence of sound engineering and simplicity.

No turnbuckle should be fitted without a toggle. Very few production boats are delivered with toggles, but the rigging does move back and forth thousands of times in a year's cruising, and the stresses upon the metal of a turnbuckle are continual. A toggle, fitted to the lower end, takes care of athwartships as well as fore-and-aft movement.

I can make no recommendations on tuning except to follow your normal practice, but remember that foresails can be cut to allow for some forestay sag. This used to be quite common in Holland, with iron rod rigging on botters, and the English sailmaker Austin Farrar has written about its effectiveness. However, it is rarely done.

2. Sails and Sail Trim

Obviously, your sail wardrobe will depend on the conditions in your regular cruising grounds. A heavy weather main makes as much sense in Southern California as does a reacher in the North Sea. Anything larger than 150 percent genoa is absurd for comfortable singlehanding, though a light reacher or "cruising spinnaker" would be easy to handle for light going. By and large, whatever working sails you have, you'll keep.

Storm sails are another matter. They are a necessity for any serious, that is to say prudent, sailor. And having them is not enough; you must know how to hoist and use them. We'll get to practice in the next chapter. Both storm jibs and trysails should be triple-stitched, roped all around and of a cloth weight equal to that of the main. Often, old cruising salts will tell you of the need for storm canvas of 12- or 14-ounce cloth. That may have been true of flax sails, but with Dacron the only thing likely to give will be the stitching. Corners must be reinforced.

The storm jib should be fitted with both foot and head pendants of wire, and really positive hanks. In gale force winds, hanks, shackles, knots—you name it—can easily be flogged open. I haven't tried them, but bronze Brummel hooks might be the answer—no moving parts and nothing to hang up on stays or sheets—aluminum ones as used on one-designs and daysailers will instantly distort.

If your sailmaker is the gung-ho racing type, and most are, you'll be assaulted with cloths, weights, stretch, warps and wefts, grooved stays and all the paraphernalia of the IOR crowd. Forget it. What you want, and need, are simple, honest sails, well cut, and with the minimum adjustments. Lots of reef points are nice, but forget about stretchy luffs, foot zippers, windows and such. Cloths should be of average weight, soft-finished.

Storm jibs should be of substantial construction with heavy stitching and chafe patches, head and foot pendants and provision for shakling or lashing to the forestay.

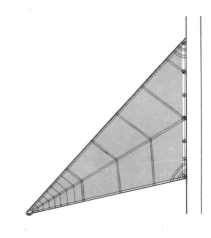

A storm trysail ideally will have its own mast track. Be sure to practice setting it in calm conditions and arrange proper leads and stern cleats.

Try to stay away from exotica. You are going to have to repair the bits and pieces by yourself. Have the headsails fitted with strong bronze piston hanks (not brass) and have them taped to the sail—it makes repairs easier. Grooved headstays are for the fully crewed yacht, not, emphatically not, for the singlehander. I have always felt, along with Ted Brewer, Bernard Heyman and a few others, that the best cruising rig is overcanvassed. You don't change down, you reef with the advent of a breeze. Mains, as mentioned before, must have at least two sets of reef points. Slab reefing is much to be preferred for the loner. The sail sets better and reefing can easily be undertaken by one soul bound to the foot of the mast. Roller reefing always sags and needs at least two to set up. If you happen to have the halyards leading to the cockpit, it is possible to arrange for reefing lines to be led aft also. Starling Burgess did it for Paul Hammond in the 1930s with *Barnswallow* and Ian Hannay used a variant on the *Galion* in the late 1960s. Once again, you have the choice of simplicity or ease of operation. Compromise and trade-offs are the keys. It's all a matter of personal preference.

If you're starting fresh, try to persuade your sailmaker to cut all the headsails with compensations for the same lead. He'll have to come aboard and measure a bit, but it means you will be able to install shorter track and will end up with less deck clutter. And the decrease in efficiency is not very great.

Roller furling and roller reefing headsails are a mixed blessing. Furling headsails sag to windward and are exposed, especially at anchor or moorings, not so much to sun deterioration but to the fury of the wind. Reefing headsails are usually more or less

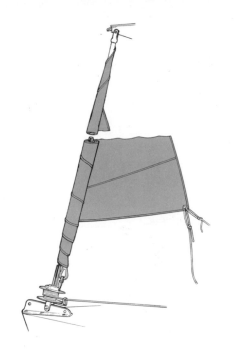

A roller-reefing headsail must be something of a compromise because it must be cut flat to function at varying degrees of roll-up. Modern versions appear to be relatively trouble-free, but be sure that you can set storm sails to a second headstay or around the existing grooved extrusion.

permanently bent on the headstay and, because they must be cut flat, are not the best as off-wind sails. If the sail or gear jams, you're stuck. And you can't well set lightweight running sails or storm canvas unless twin headstays are fitted. However,

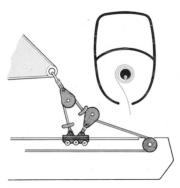

Roller-furling and reefing mainsails, such as the Hood Stoway system, solve the most dangerous parts of manual reefing because they can be totally controlled from the cockpit. However, it also means replacement of the mast and boom at considerable expense.

they're here to stay and are reasonably reliable.

Most sails are influenced in cut by the rating rules, whether IOR or local, and your sailmaker optimizes area because the rules allow it. A few square feet or meters in area don't make that much difference. However, the cut and set make all the difference in the world. For example, a flat-cut, full-hoist lapper will probably take you to windward far more effectively than a full-cut, 140

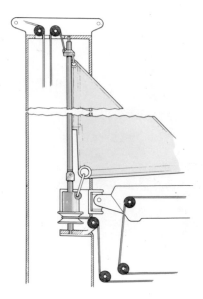

This cutaway of the interior of a Stoway mast shows the furling line and clew control line paths.

percent genoa. The similarity to a wing is of greater import in windward sails than is sheer area.

The leading edge presented to the wind is the key factor in windward performance. The higher the hoist, all other things being equal, the higher the boat will point and the greater the speed that will be attained.

On a reach, the above pretty much goes by the board. The sailmaker has to optimize both needs—area *and* efficiency, on several points of sail—to produce a usable sail, unless you wish to cart around 20 sails in the forepeak. Thus, each sail you choose should have the widest range of utility possible, correspondent with the greatest efficiency on each possible point of sail. Not an easy task.

Hoisting, lowering and trimming sail aboard a singlehanded boat can be enjoyable or downright treacherous. If you take the time to rig things right, then plan ahead and maneuver yourself and your sails with care, there's nothing to worry about. Too often, a lone sailor will panic, usually in a situation that calls for careful, deliberate action. A good example is coming into an anchorage. You rush forward, drop the jib, stuff it on one side of the foredeck, foul the anchor rode and the entire mess goes overboard, fouling the prop. You are no longer maneuverable, your engine is useless and you could well come to grief. The solution is to drop a second anchor, get the main down and unravel the mess.

However, if you had had the forethought to stow the jib properly in the first place, none of the above would have happened. Sure, push it to one side, but then tie it to the toerail or bag it and secure the bag to the pulpit. The deck is now clear for action and you can sail into that special cove, drop the anchor, back the main to set it and have a cool drink at sunset.

Too often, sail handling ends up meaning lugging lumpy bags around instead of referring to all aspects of moving the sails up, down and *on* the masts. Which brings us to the equipment and techniques of short-handed sail usage. Other than the main, which we will assume is usually left hanked on, ready to raise, of most concern to you is the appropriate sail for the foretriangle. Much of the joy and comfort of your passage depends on this. In the current fashion, headsails are large compared to the main, sometimes in a 2-to-1 ratio. These are for boats meant to rate well and go to windward well. Fine if you have a crew, not so fine if alone. If the design of your boat follows IOR guidelines, take stock. Your main will have a luff-to-foot ratio of 3 or 3½ to 1 and will be very efficient on the wind, fair on a reach and worth a half-knot downwind. On the average, for cruising in temperate areas, you will have to rely on headsails—jibs and spinnakers, or their variants. On Long Island Sound, where I spend much of my time, the winds are light and invariably from the wrong direction.

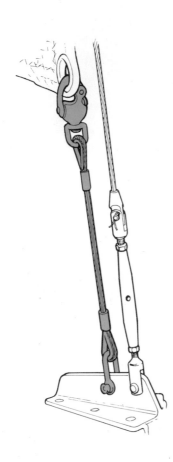

A foot pendant is highly recommended for foresails. It will improve the view forward from the cockpit as well as lessen the chance that the foresail will scoop up green water.

By and large, no cruising headsail should be a deck sweeper, and I prefer a pendant on all headsails. You won't lose much power, and if you should take green water aboard, the chances of losing that expensive jib will be lessened. Attach it to the deck or stemhead fitting with a snap shackle. I have had far too many screw shackles come undone and become a source of danger in heavy weather. A snap shackle also saves a lot of valuable time when you most need it.

You will find that any genoa more than about 140 percent of the foretriangle area will be very difficult to handle in anything over 15 to 20 knots. The bigger the boat the more this applies. No matter how powerful the winches and how well set the sail, there comes a time when you will have to douse it. Unless you are a very experienced solo sailor, your chances of lowering and bagging 400 or 500 square feet (36 or 45 square meters) of wet canvas without mangling yourself are limited. And bagging even 80 pounds (36 kilos) and getting it below can exhaust you.

The solution is to choose, especially in breezes over 12 knots or so, a sail that is one size smaller than one you would use were there crew aboard. A working jib, well cut, can be used over an enormous range. Maybe you'll lose a knot, but you won't be changing jibs every 20 minutes. Remember, you must conserve energy and strength. Though ideally you ought to attach the sheets to the jib with bowlines, for singlehanding a snap shackle, such as the Barient one especially designed for the job, makes life easier. Do not use a plunger type with a ring or lanyard that might hang up on the rigging and come undone.

Remember, if you do use a shackle, you're inviting a hit in the head by a flailing clew. A secure fastener with maximum safety is the goal.

Run the sheets back to the cockpit, through whatever fairleads or blocks (properly positioned for that particular sail) you choose, and tie figure-eight knots just short of the ends. You cannot afford a runaway sheet. The sail should still be in the bag, secured to the rail or deck. With tack and clew rigged, assess the situation. If you plan to go out under the main alone, leave it.

Time to raise the main. Cover off, stoppers off, topping lift secured, mainsheet loosened. Using a locking halyard shackle, hoist the main. A reel winch has no place on any cruising boat. If you have a wire halyard with a rope tail, make sure the wire takes three or four turns around the winch drum and cleat it. Adjust the downhaul. Go forward again and undo the mooring or prepare the anchor for hauling. If it's blowing, you can short tack up to the drop using the main alone. Sail off!

Sometimes, especially on a mooring, you may wish to get the jib up also, to give you added maneuverability. Raise the main first; then, and only then, raise the jib. It will flog. Release the mooring, move back to the cockpit and winch in the jib. Leave the main alone until you've gathered way. The headsail will supply the drive needed, and the sooner you have it drawing, the sooner you'll stop it flogging the rigging.

The key to all sail trim is simplicity. Sure, the racers have their hydraulics, grooved headstays, Barber haulers, tri-radials and crosslinked grinders, and if you wish to clutter up your deck and rig with these and others of the same ilk, go ahead. But you will discover that they do not increase boat speed or crew efficiency unless there is more than one of you . . . and there ain't.

All boats have their peculiarities, and each one will take some sailing to get the feel of what is best in different sets of circumstances. A masthead rig will take different trim techniques from a 7/8 or 3/4 rig. A ketch will take vastly different handling techniques from a sloop, and so on. But the key to sail trim is to get the most out of your sails, with the least effort, for the optimum boat speed. Your progress singlehanding will be slower than that of a fully crewed yacht, but by isolating the factors that produce the greatest speed with the least continual adjustment, you'll be able to more than hold your own.

I have seen many sailors on a reach with the genny let out short of luffing and the main tight. Now, if you think about it, this causes the main to act as a brake, not to mention that any semblance of balance is destroyed and the boat becomes more than difficult to steer. Yet hundreds of sailors who actually know better let this take place. Why? The answer seems to be that they are so concerned with genoa trim and steering, and with shouting at the crew to play the foresail sheets, that as helmsmen they neglect to trim the main.

Every book on sailing has detailed technical explanations of the slot effect. What it boils down to is that when main and foresail are trimmed with a parallel curve to their respective leeches, greater aerodynamic efficiency is achieved. Can you imagine an airplane with one wing at 90 degrees to the fusilage, and the other at 45 degrees? It boggles the mind. The dynamic principles are the same: wings through air. In the case of the boat, the wing is a bit softer, but it serves exactly the same function. You won't crash if you haven't the proper trim, but you won't move very well either.

The simplest way to cope with the slot effect, which essentially presents the most sail to the wind, is to haul in your sails as you tack, then let them out until they start to luff, finally taking them back in so that they are just short of luffing on your new course.

You'll find this strategy effective both when beating to windward and when reaching. However, as the wind comes aft of the beam, the slot disappears. You may have to contend with quartering seas, which will do their damnedest to spill wind from either

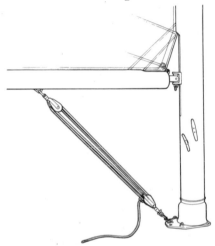

A vang tackle from the boom will eliminate twist when reaching for squared-off downwind. The purchase should be matched to sail area, and boom and deck fittings must be securely attached.

sail, usually by knocking the boat just enough off course to either overfill or empty the sails.

Secondly, and especially in light air, the apparent wind downwind is the difference between the true windspeed *and* your boat speed. You will therefore have a much harder time trimming sail with the wind aft. If it is dead astern, you have the options of sailing wing and wing or on one sail. However, since the main and jib are usually of greatly differing area, you will find it difficult to balance the boat, and steering will become more of an effort. I have found that quite often main and working jib are about the same area. Winged out, with the jib on the whisker pole and *both* sails vanged, a much more accurate course can be maintained. In a howling gale, however, I would opt for a small headsail alone. The danger of a jibe is too great. You can't cope alone prudently with steering and a wildly swinging boom.

I hope you don't try to take on too much at once. Spinnakers are without doubt the best sails off the wind. If you have the strength and skill to set one alone, fine. Most sailors, especially cruising sailors, might find them daunting. The problem is not so much setting them as dousing them. A thousand feet (300 meters) of snarled, billowing nylon is little fun. Also, to steer and trim a spinnaker at the same time is difficult because of the number of lines needed to efficiently manage the sail.

Most of the preceding discussion has had to do with headsails. After all, they compose the largest part of your inventory, cost the most and demand the most attention in setting and trimming. Mains get mistreated, creased, chafed and neglected. Yet, except in the most radical of IOR boats, they are the workhorses of sailing. After all, that's why they are called "mains."

A mainsail has to be strong, capable of being handled with just a few adjustments (very few) and infinitely versatile. You have one, and it has to suffice for all the conditions under which four or five headsails might be used. When you finally break down and order a new one, here are a few things to think about when you talk to your sailmaker.

Cloth: Often a main is constructed of much heavier cloth than is necessary. First decide where you will be cruising. If it's predominantly a light air area, you can opt for a lighter sail than might be the norm. If you plan world cruising, go for one that's heavier. Modern Dacron can take almost

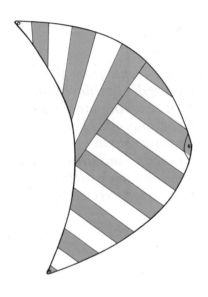

The cruising spinnaker or chute—an asymmetrical, lightweight sail used without a pole for light-air reaching or downwind work—is much easier to use than a spinnaker and is highly recommended for singlehanders and family crews.

anything (even sunlight, with the new light-stabilized cloths) and the problems that do arise have mainly to do with the stitching. If you plan any extended offshore passages, you may wish to consider a softer cloth than that used for racing. It is easier to handle, will last longer and stows in a smaller space.

Cut: Your boat has come supplied with a production main with battens. Your sailmaker has told you you'll get extra drive (and area) with battens. Everyone you know has battens. However, the only reason for using battens is to increase area, take advantage of rating rules and foul up your life. Battens break, are lost overboard, warp, tear sails and chafe the leech. No matter how well tapered and taped, how well secured in their pockets, they break and tear the sail and foul backstays.

Yet, despite all the obvious advantages, battenless, roped leeches are rarely seen, even aboard world cruisers. You may lose about 10 percent to 15 percent area this way, but you have a sail far easier to handle, with none of the disadvantages of a batten-filled main, and with distinct advantages.

Actually, on most modern boats the slight loss in area will lessen weather helm. A good cruising boat has an almost neutral helm. For a singlehander under self-steering, weather helm won't cause the boat to turn up. Furthermore, you'll have less difficulty reefing, furling and, believe it or not, trimming the sail.

Battened mains, after hard use, tend to distort just forward of the batten pockets. With a roachless main, none of this occurs and you'll find most mainsail handling a lot easier.

Many sailmakers have had little or no experience cutting such mains. Seek out a

Clew reinforcements and reinforcements at stress points will save repairs later on. Modern synthetics are preferred to leather and other easily rotted materials.

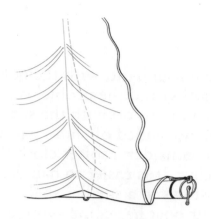

Slab reefing is probably the most popular way to shorten sail. Leech line earings must be carefully spaced and attached so the sail will set without creases when reefed.

traditional cruising specialist who knows what he's doing. You may have to undertake some research on your own and books will be of little value. The best of the lot is Jeremy Howard-Williams's *Looking at Sails.*

If you have a battened main and intend to stay with it, see that it's in good order and doesn't foul the backstay. If it does, think about having it cut down slightly. Consult your sailmaker.

Workmanship: A thorny question, dependent upon the kind of sailing you plan to do. Triple stitching, leather chafe patches and hand-sewn corners are all well and good for the traditionalist blue water man, but they also cost. Your average cruising sail, on the other hand, is less expensive and will take an awful lot of abuse and keep on going. My own working sails (first-class to start with, needless to say) are now six years old, have been used—bagged and furled—thousands of times, cleaned once a year, never repaired and still draw beautifully.

They are double-stitched, soft Dacron cloth—nothing unusual. The headsails have never been folded except by the sailmaker, after cleaning. The main is kept under cover on the boom. Stuffing a jib into a sail bag is frowned upon by everyone, but cruising sails aren't as critical as racing canvas, and no harm seems to be done.

Racing mains can be trimmed many ways. Draft, center of effort and fullness are adjustable. However, when you are alone you don't have time to concern yourself with these niceties, although certain adjustments can be useful. I'm all in favor of a downhaul, though a lot of boats are fitted with fixed goosenecks. If the luff has stretched, a downhaul gives you the opportunity to firm it up without worrying about overreaching the black band and jamming the halyard sheave. A downhaul is a great help in luff adjustment when reefing, too. Whether it's a two-part, four-part or another type of system is of little consequence as long as it works with minimum effort. Usually, and for a singlehander this is a necessity, it is cleated off with a cam cleat. A horned back-up cleat is a good idea for a blow.

Outhaul purchases are a mixed blessing. True, they allow greater finesse in draft positioning, but a well-cut cruising main shouldn't need much. I have noticed that the small sheave blocks and wire rope used for most outhauls can abrade and chafe, and a broken internal outhaul is impossible to repair at sea. A three-foot (90 cm) line, spliced to the clew ring and rove through the boom end fitting a few times, works. Tie it off with two half-hitches, and you can adjust it at will.

Topping lifts are absolutely necessary in any cruising boat, and they should be of Dacron rope or vinyl-covered wire.

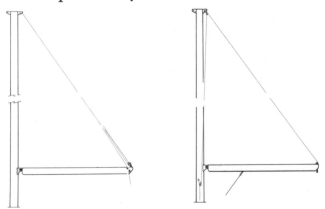

A strong and easy-to-use topping life is a necessity aboard any cruising boat. Here are two variants, one manipulated from the cockpit, one from the foot of the mast.

3. Decks and Deck Layouts

Every and any boat can be rigged for singlehanded sailing. Obviously, some are easier to handle than others, but neither size nor type of vessel should deter you from giving it a try. There is no perfect way to rig your boat, and anything I suggest is only a starting point.

So let's look at what you've got hanging on the mooring or tied to the dock. Chances are it's a sloop, somewhere between 28 and 35 feet (8.4 and 10.5 meters) LOA. It's got a forestay, a backstay, uppers and double lowers—inboard rudder, trunk cabin, a few winches, a few cleats, slab reefing, topping lift, working sails and a genny complete the picture.

Standard wisdom has it that all sheets and halyards should be led aft to the cockpit for efficient singlehanding. This is a super idea if you happen to be lazy, or particularly fond of the cockpit. However, by setting up a

Leading all running rigging—halyards, sheets, lifts, guys, reefing line—aft to the cockpit may seem practical, but in reality you must always go forward to untangle something. Leading halyards aft to winches on the coachroof at the forward end of the cockpit, however, usually works fine.

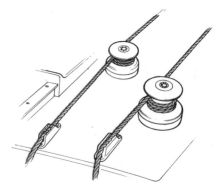

configuration of winches, stoppers and blocks, you tend to clutter the deck, set up hazards all over the place and generally complicate matters.

Now, don't take this as gospel. There are occasions when having everything at hand can be a blessing: a full gale offshore or a tight maneuvering situation, for instance. What you have to consider is the extent to which you wish to compromise. For every line led back to the cockpit, at least two blocks will be necessary, not to mention those cleats, stoppers and winches. The major problem is not really obstruction; it's chafe. For example, an internal main halyard can exit the mast through a block, pass through a turning block on deck, wend its way through a couple of fairleads and around a winch, and end up belayed over the edge of the coachroof on a proper cleat (more on this later). Depending on how you count, that's six or seven chafe points. If you leave the whole mess on the mast, you will have to contend with the exit block, a winch and a cleat. And don't for a minute think you don't have to worry about chafe with winches and cleats. They take their toll. The nasty fact is that replacing a halyard at sea can be a lot more difficult than clambering up to the mast now and then. But whatever you do, you'll have to weigh efficiency, safety and ease of operation with that most important of seamanlike dictates: keep it simple.

If there are to be any recurring themes in this book, simplicity is the one most likely to be hammered home. Every piece of equipment added on board becomes a contributing factor in the application of Murphy's law. Furthermore, modern gear is costly and increasingly sophisticated. When it works, it's lovable; when it doesn't, you end up with a boatload of expensive paperweights. And the designers and manufacturers are not really to blame. The sea has spent thousands of years destroying

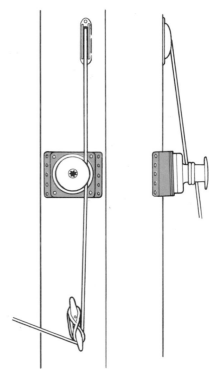

Internal halyards secured at the mast should lead from exit sheaves around a winch and to a slightly offset cleat, as shown here. The cleat should be mounted at least a foot (30 cm) below the winch to allow for leverage and tensioning, as well as to work the winch handle.

whatever man has placed in its embrace. No matter how hard our alloys, how resistant our synthetics, the sea has it in for us. Without constant care, nothing, absolutely nothing, can survive the ravages of salt, wind and water.

Buy the best and buy the least. It may not make your local chandler happy, but you'll be glad of it in a few months, not to mention years, later.

Increasingly, production boats come with deck-stepped masts. The compression is borne by the bulkhead underneath. For most sailing this works just fine; it solves the problems of mast boot leaks, keeps the mast out of the cabin and, if the mast goes overboard, it can be retrieved (you hope) with little damage. That bulkhead, however, is very vulnerable. Ideally it should be fully glassed to hull and deckhead, the doorway through to the forecabin (the area of greatest stress) should be oval and the frame or surround should be laminated. Even then, potential weaknesses abound.

If possible, find a boat with mast stepped on the keel, and a keel with substantial floors and support. Whichever you have, see to it that there is proper drainage for the foot of the mast and some way to adjust fore-and-aft rake. One further option might be mentioned, one not often seen on American boats but popular in Europe: the tabernacle. Irving Johnson's last *Yankee* was equipped this way, as is Mike Peyton's ketch. Advantages are total freedom from cranes and fixed bridges, and the ability to lower away and undertake repairs yourself.

At a few feet (about 1 meter) up from the base will be a cluster of winch pads. These ought to be slightly offset from a beam-on position, made of aluminum or stainless steel,

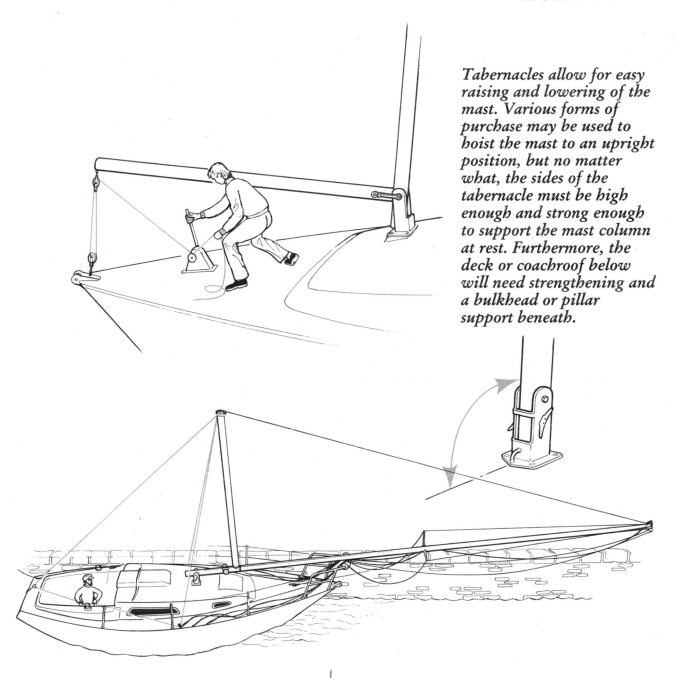

Tabernacles allow for easy raising and lowering of the mast. Various forms of purchase may be used to hoist the mast to an upright position, but no matter what, the sides of the tabernacle must be high enough and strong enough to support the mast column at rest. Furthermore, the deck or coachroof below will need strengthening and a bulkhead or pillar support beneath.

and either welded or attached with self-tapping machine screws, with proper insulating gaskets for both pad and screws. Galvanic corrosion is a real problem, and chances are the mast, not the pad, will be weakened. Also, keep the fittings to a minimum. Too many winches and cleats weaken mast structure. After all, the mast is just a hollow aluminum tube, and if you drill

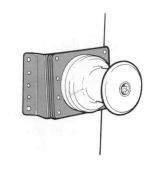

Galvanic corrosion can be caused all too easily by mounting dissimilar metals together. Winches, winch pads and the mast must all be isolated by nonconductive gaskets—made of neoprene or similar materials—and the same holds true for fasteners. Also, try to stagger winches on either side of the mast so that no one area is pierced by many mounting holes.

A vast array of winches is available on the market, from single-speed, bottom-handled to 3-speed electric. For smaller boats, bottom-handled ratcheting winches have much to offer: ease of operation, no separate handle to get lost and speed in throwing off turns. However, they cannot work fast. A top-handled winch can supply greater power and can be had in a much greater variety of sizes and gear ratios. Drum materials can be glassfiber-filled nylon, tufnol, aluminum, bronze or stainless steel.

it full of holes in one area you jeopardize the ultimate strength of a vertical strut under compression. Personally, I have no winches on the mast. I use tackles for setting up halyards, along with downhauls for final tensioning. I am in the minority, though, and if you do have halyard winches on the mast, make sure the jib winch is either higher or lower than the main winch and on the opposite side (less chance of localized stress). Cleats should be below the winch, by at least a foot, angled to allow for easing and stopping the line. Fastening procedures are the same as for the winch pads.

Another alternative is clustering the winches on deck at the base of the mast. If you are going to use winches, this may be the best solution. It allows easier handling in heavy weather (your center of gravity is lower), keeps anything from weakening the mast structure and allows you to use the winches for other purposes—for warping alongside from amidships, as an anchor winch and so on.

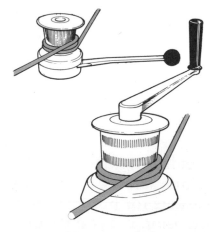

The last possibility, and the one most beloved by singlehanders, especially the ocean-crossing variety, is leading everything, absolutely everything, back to the cockpit. This involves all the clutter and mechanical complications mentioned above, but it does allow for absolute ease and safety, in that you almost never have to leave the cockpit . . . perfect for the sedentary, but also immensely energy conserving and safe. If you opt for this, single winches on either side of the companionway, with stoppers just ahead on the coachroof, is the most economical and efficient way of doing things. Don't forget that winches are heavy, so the fewer up high, the less windage and the lower the center of gravity.

You may have noticed we're working our way back to the cockpit. Here's where you spend most of your time, relaxing, drinking, eating, making love, screaming at your wife/mistress/children/crew—and actually sailing. No cockpit is ideal, a reality you will just have to learn to live with. If it's big enough to lounge around in, it's too big for ultimate seaworthiness. If it's too deep, being pooped can be dangerous. If you allow yourself to buy a vessel without a bridgedeck, you run the risk not only of taking green water below but also of weakening the deck structure. With a tiller you crowd things, and with a wheel you add to mechanical complexity, as most wheels are placed with an eye to a crew operating winches and other contrivances. My own prejudice (not carried out to perfection on my own boat) would be for a setup similar to that of the *Great Dane*, a 28-foot (8.4 meters) sloop of docile performance but great thoughtfulness, designed by the late Aege Utzon. The rudder is transom-hung, the helmsman's seat is raised, four large cockpit drains keep things dry, the winches can be operated by either helmsman or crew, the mainsheet comes to hand at the helm, and the compass can be read from any part of the rather small cockpit.

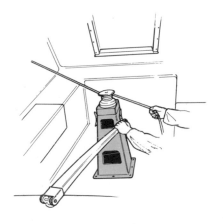

One possible cockpit layout for singlehanders is a central pedestal with a single winch. It saves money, allows for clean coamings and puts everything at hand.

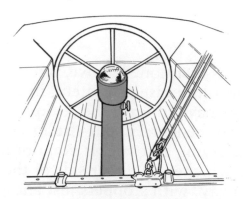

In a wheel-steered yacht, having the mainsheet traveller run directly in front of the wheel keeps control with the helmsman. Likewise, primary winches should be nearby, not forward as in crewed yachts.

The *Great Dane* cockpit is perfect for a small singlehanded boat for *me*. Maybe not for you. As with cheesecakes and art, no one agrees, or has to, on matters of taste; and boats are irrational mistresses. Jim Crawford, who built *Agantyr* and sailed her singlehanded for long distances, had the boat designed with no cockpit at all, though he was perhaps more interested in ultimate seaworthiness than most of us are. However, However, since the aft end of any boat we will use is going to have a well in it, let's go about using it as best we can. For the singlehander, the primary concern is having everything at hand, as in a good galley. The less effort expended getting from one activity to another, the better. The key word is activity, for you alone can decide what is most important to you and what is done most often. Thus my notion of keeping halyards at the mast. How often do you hoist sails, in comparison to trimming sheets or moving the tiller or wheel? Just as you have the radio below (to keep it safe, and dry as well) because it is not used every five minutes, so you need the compass in the optimal viewable spot.

In the Trades, a boat can be allowed to sail itself for vast stretches. Most of us, cruising for a few weeks in coastal waters, can't experience the luxury of steady winds—and untouched sails. We can't inspect rigging at our leisure and sit in the cockpit working fancy rope patterns for galley mats. Sailing is fun, but it is work too. Don't forget that. You plan your landside work and the procedures to accomplish it best, so you must plan your sailing. You should know beforehand the steps necessary to change a headsail or anchor the boat. And you should practice. You couldn't become a concert pianist without practice, and you cannot become a good sailor without practice, either. I have spent years arguing with my racing friends that seamanship is not getting the most out of a boat to windward but getting the boat and crew to their destination safely. It is waterborne management. And it is a collection of techniques . . . none of which comes naturally. Practice, practice, practice. We all know the performance is better than the rehearsals, but unless you know your lines by heart, you won't be able to bring it off. We all know the drill about throwing a life preserver overboard, jibing, and retrieving it. On a calm day, try throwing your least favorite kid overboard and try getting him back on board!

What, you ask, does this have to do with singlehanding, and the cockpit? If you are alone in the cockpit, you must be able to do anything required without having to take the time to find things, set up devices, or plan maneuvers. Contingency planning must be done, and the logical place to start is with the arrangement and modification of the cockpit.

Let's begin at the bottom and work our way up. Production boats, with the exception of a very few, have inadequate cockpit drains. Assuming you get pooped, how much water would the cockpit hold? 50 gallons (190 litres)? 100 gallons (380 litres)? At 8 pounds (3.6 kilos) per gallon, that's a lot of weight dragging the stern. If your boat has the standard two ¾- to 1½-inch (2- to 4-cm) drains, it will not empty fast enough to bring up the stern before another wave fills the well again. This can not only soak you and everything else, it can bloody well sink your ship. I feel that four 1½-inch (4 cm) drains should be installed, one at each corner, flush with the sole and with crossbars over them. Grates

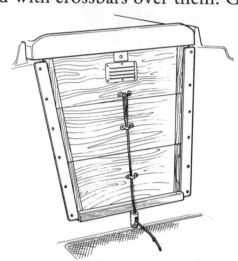

For any offshore passage, some means of securing the duckboards for the companionway hatch is a necessity. In the event of pooping or capsize, flooding will occur if the boards are not secured. Some variants allow for operation from either cockpit or cabin.

obstruct more than they allow through. The drains should drain overboard through double-clamped reinforced hoses and seacocks that can be reached without jeopardizing the watertight integrity of the cockpit.

In boats with cockpits extending to the transoms, direct ports through the stern above the waterline are best, with neoprene flaps fitted to the outside of the transom to keep the water from entering.

Next up, usually to starboard of the helm, are the engine controls. Today these are clever single-lever arrangements. I remember that, in my father's boat, to shift from anything, a bronze deckplate was flipped open, a long, lethal bronze lever inserted and brute force applied, usually resulting in permanent damage to ego, body or boat, or combinations thereof. These controls need little in the way of care except lubrication and tightening now and then. However, the accompanying electrical connections for ignition, switches, starting plugs and such are highly vulnerable to water, spray, mist, bumps and knocks. If they are behind a Plexiglas panel, the panel should be gasketed and capable of being securely fastened. Instruments should be high enough (especially engine instruments) to be both visible and clear of any volume of water that might fill the well.

When you bought your boat, the salesman no doubt told you about the wonderfully capacious cockpit lockers: "They'll hold everything." They probably do. And they should not only be gasketed and sealable against being thrown open in a knockdown, they should also be organized. All those lines, fenders, sails, spares, oars, anchors and objects best described as junk are ostensibly there for a purpose.

Stock boat builders do not generally do anything with locker space. It is too damn expensive. Thus you are left with one, two or three holes, deep holes at that, that have an uncanny way of collecting water in those corners where chain rusts away or awnings mildew and molder. Just imagine being forced to live in a cockpit locker for 24 hours. Enough said?

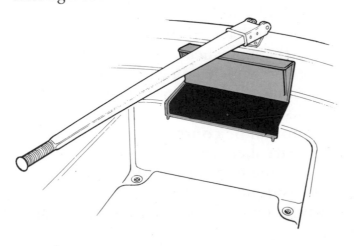

Lazarettes are useful for stowing an assortment of gear. However, they should have removeable bottoms and be divided. Otherwise, smaller bits will drop into the bilges and you will never be able to find anything. Also, the lids should be strongly hinged, gasketed and capable of being positively secured and locked.

Lockers should be divided horizontally and vertically, with a grate for the bottom division to keep large items out of the bilge water. Then make vertical partitions to segregate odds and ends so that what you use most is easily accessible, what you rarely use is easy to get to, and what you never use can be thrown out! Try to keep the aft end of the lockers free of anything but fenders and other such lightweight gear. Heavy items drag down the stern, making for hard steering and sluggish handling. Don't put the outboard motor in the lazaret or afterlocker. Every added bit of weight hampers sailing characteristics, and way aft is the worst place possible to put anything.

The most important gear in the cockpit, as far as the singlehander is concerned, are the mainsheet and jibsheet arrangements. Both must be at hand to the helmsman, for the lone sailor must be able to control all, with minimum movement and as little fouling as possible, while at the helm.

Cockpit arrangement is the area in which most stock boats fall short of the ideal. Nine out of ten boats on the water are billed as cruiser/racers. They are designed for families and Sunday around-the-buoy charges. They are built with production-line economy in mind. When the occasion for singlehanding arises, you find you have to run forward to trim the jib, run back to the helm, reach around for the mainsheet, and generally waste time and effort which you cannot afford, alone, accomplishing the most necessary and simple tasks.

The main can be controlled most simply by a multipart sheet running through blocks at the end of the boom to a cam cleat on the afterdeck—simple, but does not offer much in the way of control, especially in heavy air.

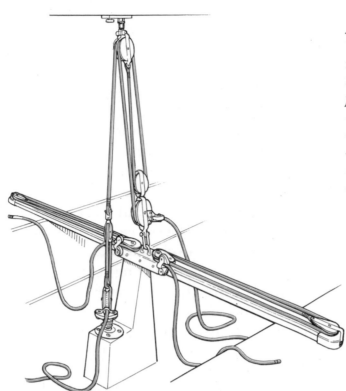

Mainsheet traveller system. This example is ideal, running fully athwartships, the stops adjustable by purchases and cam cleats, the mainsheet double-ended. Not often seen, double-ended mainsheets allow both the helmsman and crew to make adjustments.

Better yet, run the sheet to a track-mounted roller-bearing car running clear across the after end of the cockpit. Note "clear across." The longer the track, the easier it is to control mainsail twist. The track should be fitted with extra-heavy end stops, not those little nylon jobbies, and the car should be equipped with control lines leading to cam cleats at either end. Spring-loaded stops are difficult, not to mention dangerous, to adjust in any sort of breeze. Besides, the control lines give added leverage, and any mechanical aid is appreciated when you're alone.

Two other possibilities exist. The first involves running the track across the bridge deck. This is especially useful in a tiller-steered boat. You won't have to reach behind the tiller. Here the sheets are attached to the boom by means of a bail, internal or external. With a long, heavy boom, a tripartite bail system is preferable, in that it spreads the strains. Try to get the lead as vertical as possible, at a right angle to the deck, when the boom is on the centerline. The second, and even better, alternative is a double-ended sheet, with one end leading to a deck-mounted traveler, the other through a block at either end of the boom. If aft, a cam cleat holds; if forward, the line goes through a block on deck, back to the end of the coachroof and another cam cleat (with a winch in between if you've got yourself a hefty mainsheet purchase).

No matter what arrangement you decide upon, make sure that the sheet can be both hauled in and released from the helm position. And use nothing smaller than ⅜-inch (2 cm) Dacron. Anything smaller is impossible to grip under strain with any degree of comfort. Also, use a sheet long enough to permit the boom to swing to a 90-degree angle to the mast.

The power of a purchase is directly proportional to the number of its parts. A 5- or 6-part tackle is preferred for a mainsheet on a larger yacht, sometimes in conjunction with a winch.

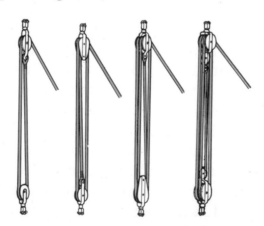

Often, especially on West Coast boats and on Hickleys, you'll see a traveler mounted on the coachroof over the companionway hatch. This is a super arrangement except for two little oddments: one, the sheet terminates at the aft end of the coachroof; and two, it may be very difficult to mount a dodger, which is absolutely vital for any hard going to windward.

The options for controlling the jibsheets are legion. If anything, there are too many possibilities—winches, leads, cleats; tracks, cars, blocks, single and double sheets, purchases, and so on. In principle, all you need is something to give you the mechanical advantage to haul in the sail, lead it true for optimum shape and secure it. Sounds simple, yet the modern ocean racer has made the handling of headsails into a game for engineers and mathematicians. It needn't be.

Starting at the clew of the sail, bend on the sheets with bowlines. Sure, shackles are easier. They can also do a splendid job of bashing across your skull when you go forward to change sails. Bowlines are easy to tie, easy to untie. Simple, remember? The options for sheet leads are usually taken care of at the factory: tracks of aluminum or stainless steel, with blocks or cars sliding along their inadequate length. These tracks should be angled, at least 6 feet (1.8 meters) long (on a 30-foot (9 meters) boat) and through-bolted. A strong stop at the aft end is a good idea. The slide of the car or block carriage is easiest to use if spring-loaded, but be sure a lanyard is attached. It's damn hard to pull a plunger on a tossing deck with wet hands.

Another possibility is individual deck pads with snapshackle snatch blocks for leads. Such an arrangement keeps the deck clear, although, of course, the positions are extremely important and you cannot allow for infinite adjustments. On small boats, under 25 feet (7.5 meters) or so, consider using fairleads rather than blocks. They are cheaper, need no maintenance and can be track-mounted. They make no noise either.

One of the omissions on all boats—all—
are leads for storm sails. You don't have a
storm jib? You may not need it for 10 years,
but when you do, there is no alternative.
We'll talk about this more in the chapter on
sails, but for the moment, let me suggest you
hoist the spitfire, work out the leads for it
and get them attached—very securely—to the
deck. Padeyes will suffice, but the best
solution is the screw-in deck block made by
Gibb or Schafer. When the block proper is
removed, all you have is a narrow, flush-
mounted deck plate. No stubbed toes, no sail
snaggers.

Assuming you have the sheet led properly,
roughly allowing the sail to be hauled in flat
to windward with no apparent distortions,
you've got to have some power to actually
get it in, and for singlehanding, you have to
consider the winches you will choose most
carefully. First, they must be large, as large as
your mounting areas and budget will allow.
Of course, you shouldn't get carried away,
but one or even two sizes larger than
recommended isn't a bad idea. I happen to
like aluminum barrel winches rather than
bronze. The cost differential isn't so great any
more, and they are much lighter. This is not
simply an advantage to top-hamper weight. If
you have to repair a pawl or such in a
seaway, a bronze drum can hurt a lot more
than an aluminum one—and go overboard
more easily!

Winches available on the market: single,
two- and three-speed, self-ratcheting, top or
bottom handle, self-tailing, self-cleating and
so on. I must admit to a weakness for bottom
handle winches for singlehanding—no handle
to lose overboard, easier to cast off sheets.
Also, they are slower in operation and
usually less powerful. However, speed isn't

of great importance and the loss of power can be compensated for with a larger winch. Unfortunately, the only ones available are by Gibb (in three sizes, for boats up to 32 feet or 9.6 meters), Barton, and Murray (in many variations). If you have a smaller ship, consider these. Remember, winch handles are expensive, and bottom handle winches are especially handy for use as halyard haulers. No grappling forward with a handle, no stowage problems at the mast. These are single-speed, very simple winches, with ratchet handles. You can't haul in as fast, but you shouldn't have to, and alone you couldn't anyway.

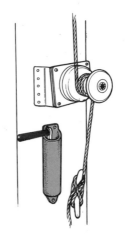

Next are the workhorses: single- or multi-speed winches with top handles. What I've said about bottom handle winches also applies to these, plus the fact that the higher gear ratios of the second or third speed allow for greater leverage in heavy going. All the major manufacturers put out good products, and they all work just fine. Just remember, you get what you pay for.

Self-tailing and -cleating winches are a commercial development of the mid-1970s. They are marvelously sophisticated mechanical devices. All you do is turn the handle. They grab the rope, keep it moving and hold it. What more could you want? For a singlehander they seem to be the ideal solution. I have my doubts. These jobbies are complicated. That means maintenance and added bother. Also, they grab the rope, causing chafe. No matter what anyone says, additional friction points mean added wear. Finally, they are self-cleating. Since the winch becomes the final resting place for the sheet, heavy strains are put on the fastenings and coaming. I have seen a well-fastened winch rip off its fiberglass base in a gale. Carrying

Winch handles have a nasty habit of falling overboard. Considering their cost, some means of securing them at hand is almost a necessity. PVC holders, such as these, are by far the easiest to install and the least likely to foul lines. They should have drain holes in the bottom.

the strain back to a cleat is, in my book, imperative. If you like them, by all means get a pair, but be careful about installation and have backup cleats, abaft the winches.

Try to install the winch so the sheet leads to the winch from below, at an angle of a few degrees. Otherwise, you'll end up with riding turns and fouled lines. Watch out for potential snags along the lead, and make sure the lead to the cleats is as straight as possible. It used to be fashionable to mount cleats outboard of the coamings—difficult to reach and chafe producing. It is better that we have wide, molded coamings these days.

The number of abominations passed off as cleats today is astounding. Unequivocally, the best cleats are those of the old Herreshoff design—hollow molded, with a four-bolt base. They hold better and chafe less than anything else on the market. Clam cleats slip under extreme strain, cam cleats break and jam cleats can't accept turns.

Many devices are available for securing lines. The most reliable is the double-horned Herreshoff cleat. It holds more turns, will not abrade the line and can be used for many applications. Line stoppers are best mounted forward of winches, so the winch can be used for multiple tasks. Cam cleats will hold light loads. I dislike clam cleats, frankly, and would only consider them to secure non−load-bearing lines.

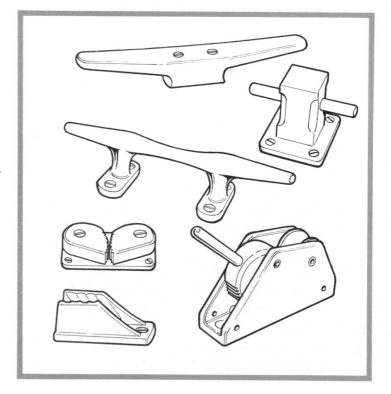

Now, other patterns exist: the so-called sailboat cleats, horn cleats, wood cleats, wood and metal cleats. They all work, but they all add to chafe to some degree or another. Plastic cleats break, but Tufnol is okay if you can find a good shape. Basically what you want is something with smooth edges, the capacity to take at least two complete turns and a base that is broad enough to take the strains imposed upon the entire structure.

4. Down Below

At last we can get to the comfort and safety of the cabin, where you sleep, eat, navigate and perform those various private functions so necessary to the maintenance of the human body and spirit. In the past several years, especially since the explosion of sailing upon the popular imagination, "down below" has become synonymous with selling genuine teak, shaggy carpets, cathedral-like headroom, head compartments for orgies and galleys for "gourmet" meals. No one tells the newcomer to the sport that none of the above really is important to the pleasures of sailing and, in fact, a great deal of it is positively detrimental to the enjoyment of a cruise.

Let's start with the requirements of the singlehander: a secure berth, an easy-to-work galley and a dry, stable platform for navigation. And, of course, something with a hole in the top to act as a toilet. In a moderate-sized vessel of standard layout this means a galley to port and a quarter berth and chart table to starboard. The rest of the ship is luxury. All the essential elements for existence are at hand to the companionway, and you can then use the forepeak for sails (it is of dubious value for much else anyway).

The above takes care of your needs whether on a coastal hop or a transoceanic passage. The saloon becomes an in-port living room, the head compartment can be used for whatever and you live happily. I say this about the head because it usually is too far from the cockpit for singlehanding. If you have to get on deck in a hurry, you have to fight through the cabin. Much easier to use is the old cedar bucket, providing it is legal where you sail. (Actually, any bucket will do, as long as you remember to fill it one-third with seawater.) Also, it has the advantage of being useful anywhere.

The chart table can be made more practicable, if of the usual athwartships variety, with a removable fiddle at its outboard edge, a red light above and good holders for pencils, protractors, dividers and such. If much of the quarter berth extends

Chart tables below are of dubious value to the singlehander when underway. A better idea is a folding cockpit-mounted table with a hinged sheet of rigid clear plastic or Lexan under which a chart may be kept reasonably dry and upon which courses can be marked with a grease pencil.

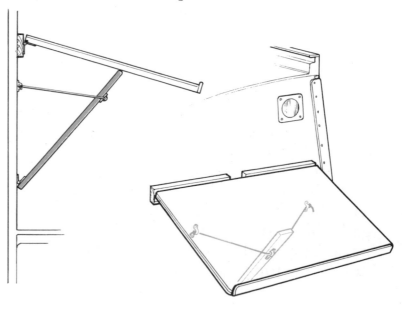

past the companionway ladder, a leecloth becomes necessary, and a plastic sheeting rain shield can be a godsend. Oilskin stowage and boot stowage might profitably be fitted behind the companionway ladder or to one side. A good idea is to fit racks or shelves either side of the main hatch *inside* for binoculars, flares, fire extinguisher and first aid kit.

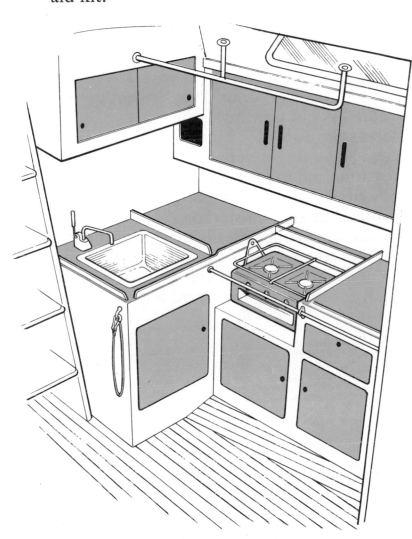

A well-designed galley is one way to make cruising more pleasant. However, few stock yachts are equipped with the safety features most needed: a strong support bar in front of the stove, high fiddles with provision for cleaning, a galley belt, and overhead handrails. Since you need both hands for most cooking tasks, the belt may be found to be most useful.

The stove should be gimbaled, with room to swing 35 to 40 degrees. It must have rails and adjustable pot holders, and the stove recess should be lined with asbestos-insulated stainless steel. Try to keep all edges of everything well rounded. I remember a cruise on which I was pitched against the galley counter in only a moderate sea and managed to crack two ribs. A safety belt helps, as do proper handholds—vertical, horizontal, everywhere imaginable. You should be able to travel the length and breadth of the cabin with a strong handhold—one that can be gripped through or totally around. Recesses and scalloped drawer pulls don't count!

Also in the galley department: if your sink is the standard 6 inches (15 cm) deep, tear it out and find one at least 9 (23 cm), preferably 12 inches (30.5 cm) deep. They are not easy to come by, but they make the most secure holders imaginable for bottles, jars, pans and dishes. Make sure it will drain before you invest time and money. I have spent many happy hours in one boat that gurgled and half-filled the sink on starboard tack. Another worthwhile idea is to get rid of the plumbing completely, fill in the through-hull, and cut out the counter to take a plastic wash basin, or, better yet, a standard bucket. When

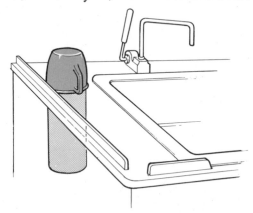

Designer and illustrator Bruce Bingham came up with this idea. Simply bore a hole in the galley counter to hold a thermos bottle securely. You will always have hot water for drinks and there is no chance of the bottle rolling across the floorboards.

you're through washing up, lift it out and empty it overboard. With a little ingenuity you will be able to rid yourself of any number of "modern conveniences," all designed to put holes in the bottom of the boat and to clog with alarming frequency.

The cabin sole is your terra firma for the passage. Make it worthy of your feet. Carpets have absolutely no place on a seagoing boat. They slip, soak up water, and get in the way when you have to dive into the bilges. Unvarnished teak makes the best sole, though it is heavy and expensive. Teak-faced plywood is a good alternative. Whatever you use, do not varnish it! It looks pretty varnished but makes about the most dangerous flooring man could create. Better a nonskid paint. Be sure to bevel the edges of the removable floorboards about 15 degrees; otherwise, when they swell you'll never get them up. Lifting rings should be installed, set flush. You should not need a chisel to lift a hatch. If you can arrange gratings at the foot of the companionway and in the head compartment, all the better.

Underway, even more than at anchor, ventilation is of prime importance. After all, it's nice to be able to breathe. Most American boats are fitted with forward-opening hatches, despite the well-known fact that air is sucked in in reverse. Aft-opening hatches permit circulation beating to windward . . . in the rain. When it's really pouring, and battening down is imperative, Dorade boxes are the simplest answer, as well as Vetus-type ventilators and sunshine boxes. The last are a Gary Mull innovation, and they seem to work quite well. At sea, centerline hatches are best. Anything off center is asking for trouble in the event of a knockdown.

Headroom is another cry at the boat show or showroom. Phil Rhodes once said, "You don't have standing headroom in a Cadillac." The only time I've ever really missed it is when at anchor in heavy rain. Otherwise, unless you're an inveterate pacer standing headroom is a luxury, though it's nice in the

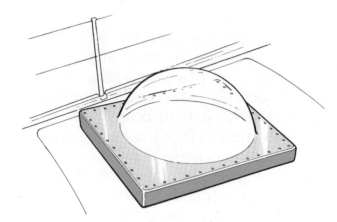

One way to increase light, beadroom and visibility is to install a dome in the cabin top or in a hatch. The companionway, provided no garage is fitted, may be the best place for this. With the self-steering at work, you can stay below and see around 360 degrees just by popping up beneath the dome. Handholds on either side below are a good addition.

galley and heads. Chuck Paine's little 26-footer (7.8 meters) *Frances* has 6 feet (1.8 meters) in the doghouse and sitting room everywhere else, yet it is one of the most delightful small cruising boats around. You come below, take off your oilies, put on the kettle and check the charts, having to stoop only to go forward to the head or the forepeak berth. Anything over 30 feet (9 meters) and you'll have the headroom unless you are *very* tall. If that's the case, either be very rich and get a big boat or else lie down.

Assuming you're pretty much stuck with a stock design, how you customize it depends on personal preferences and manias. The important questions to ask yourself are: Does it add to safety? Does it add to efficiency? Does it add to comfort? Most additions add to comfort. Now, I'm all for comfort, but there are limits. And comfort is relative. In heavy weather, warm dry socks are a luxury. In the Caribbean, a freshwater shower can be worth four hundred pairs of socks.

My friend Bruce Bingham, who is certainly one of the most experienced sailors and designers around, believes that only solid leeboards are viable. I, on the other hand, prefer cloth. Why? In the days when sea berths were just wide enough to wedge yourself in and have room for the natural expansion of the lungs, a solid board worked great. But builders realized that most people sleep only at anchor. They made the bunks 2 feet (60 cm) or more wide. On a hot night, under the enchantment of tropic skies, you need plenty of room to toss and turn in. At sea the opposite is true. With a wide bunk, in any sort of seaway, you'll be tossed from side to side. With a solid board, you court a chance of bruised chest, mangled limbs or a squashed nose. Cloth is resilient—as, presumably, are you—and will offer greater ultimate protection, provided it is properly sewn and installed.

A "proper" leeboard is made of heavy weight canvas or Acrilan, with edges doubled and sewn and grommets sewn in (*not* tacked through) on all corners and along both bottom and top edges. The top lines are tied to through-bolted fittings in the cabin top or to the handrails if these exist. The stresses caused by an average body hurtling even 8 inches (20 cm) can be astonishing.

When not in use, the whole kit stows under the bunk cushion. Unlike wood, it doesn't warp, rattle, splinter or add weight. It is also much cheaper.

If any locker door is equipped with friction or magnetic catches, carefully unscrew them, carry them topside and drop them overboard to sink into a well-deserved grave. When a locker door springs open, the contents have a tendency to be jettisoned with cruel force. A winch handle hitting you in the head is not amusing. Sometimes it is fatal. The simplest and most secure catches I know of are the old-fashioned button catch, either wood or bronze. The type that involves inserting your finger into a hole and pulling it looks neat, but, if the boat lurches, your finger stands a good chance of coming out mangled and broken.

Locker doors are best installed with the hinges along the bottom edge, for less strain on the hinges and catch. Another good alternative is sliding doors. Popular on Scandinavian boats, they solve the catch problem by doing away with it in toto. And though messier looking, open-faced bins with netting or shock cord preventers are simplest of all and allow fastest access.

Now the problem of actually functioning below while heeled. A lot of designers and builders seem to think that stuffing the

One way to increase security, especially when ascending or descending the companionway steps, is to have harness clip-on points both above and below. These plastic-covered wire lines running force-and-aft in the saloon are adapted from a suggestion by Des Sleightholme.

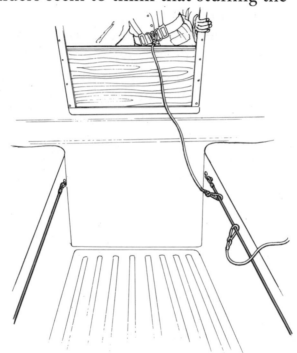

requisite number of berths, galley, head and a few shelves into the shell of a boat creates a seagoing environment. Not so! If you were to take a small table, place a mug of water on it and start to tilt it, at a tilt of about 20 degrees the mug would start to slide. If you also kicked the table, the mug would be flung off and would soak the carpet. If that were a cup of coffee and you were bracing yourself against the table's edge, you would have been scalded. Des Sleighthome, editor emeritus of *Yachting Monthly*, wrote a very perceptive article about "angles of heel" and brought up some obvious (and rarely noted) points:

First, every flat surface must have stout and high fiddles to prevent athwartship movement beyond the confines of that surface. An inch or two will work in calm conditions, but when the going gets rough, 3- or 4-inch-high (8 or 10 cm) rails are much more practical and useful. As long as they work, they'll do. Nice teak is standard, but a Nicholson yacht I saw recently has aluminum fiddles in the galley, with rounded corners and lapped top edges. Very handsome and very practical too.

Remember, you're alone and can't hand anyone anything, so be prepared to place things where they will remain until you need them again. Fiddled surfaces or bins are the answer. You very rarely see bins on boats these days, yet they are perhaps the most efficient means of storing things in odd corners. They should have removable covers and some way to fasten the cover securely. In a knockdown, not only will the cover fly but any contents (like the sextant) will follow, usually with scarifying results.

Second, handholds ought to be as obvious as bannisters on stairs. I was recently cruising on a very expensive production yacht, of impeccable basic construction. Below was not a single rail, pillar, or post, and it was a beamy yacht with a very wide sole. The current trend toward open spaces is fine for latent claustrophobics, but ghastly at sea. You can walk across the kitchen for an onion, but being thrown across the galley into a distant chart table hurts!

If you can, install handholds so you can walk the entire length of the interior without

releasing one before you get to the next.
Another of Sleighthome's suggestions is a
length of nonstretch Dacron strung from a
bulkhead or pillar to a cockpit cleat. I've tried
it this season and it works. Easy to grab,
cheap and quickly rigged, and removable.
Another example of the obvious that you
tend never to think of.

5. Planning and the Avoidance of Fatigue

The greatest enemy of the solo sailor is
fatigue. No ifs, ands or buts. Tiredness causes
unclear thinking, which in turn leads to
unbelievable stupidity—even in experienced
sailors. I remember once sailing to Nantucket
from City Island. The seas were lumpy, it
was cold, I had been on watch for more than
14 hours. Not only was my navigation off—I
was 5 miles (8 km) too far to the south—but
I had started to imagine I was sailing uphill. I
decided to put into Menemsha Pond and was
promptly rammed against the pier by the
currents running inside the entrance. So
much for my seamanship!

On an offshore passage, sleep is possible,
when far enough away from shipping lanes,
lee shores and navigational hazards. But in
confined waters, and at any distance less than

50 miles (80 km) or so from land, a constant watch must be kept not only on the boat and its components but also of *everything* around. Water, sky, buoys, ships, landmarks. And that watch must be constant. Actually, the human mind is ill-suited to concentration aboard a yacht, unless trained for just that

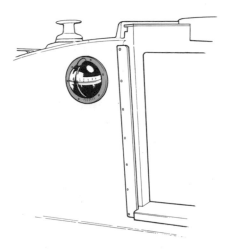

Having the steering compass mounted at eye level and protected from glare and hard objects makes a helmsman's job that much easier. Ideally, as in this arrangement, a second compass should be mounted to starboard of the companionway.

task. Every time you introduce a new crew member to the dubious joys of sailing, he or she is given a turn at the helm. The percentage of "concentrators" who can keep a course for more than a minute or two is very low. They look at the gulls, at other boats, at the topless beauty on the big ketch. But can they keep their minds plastered on sails and wind shifts? Not easily, unless they have grasped the fact that much more important matters are at hand (and eye). You may have been sailing for 20 years and never have been in the position of having to understand the magnitude or multiplicity of tasks involved in sailing because others have taken responsibility for them.

Fatigue is not merely due to standing watch. It can arise from a complex combination of factors. Steady sun, heavy meals and booze, combined with the routine tasks aboard any yacht, are enough to cause most any sailor to feel tired and draggy and to lose the concentration and reflexes needed to make sharp and fast judgments.

How do you prevent fatigue? And what can you do about it once it's come on? The answer to both questions is simple . . . sleep. However, there are times when sleep is the one thing you cannot do, no matter what.

It helps to start a sail fresh. If you plan to start at dusk—something to be recommended, since you can then make port during daylight—sleep the day before. Stay up the preceding night if necessary, but try not to be up for more than a few hours before casting off.

As the body wakes up, it burns energy at an astonishing rate, especially when engaged in strenuous tasks. If possible, have everything aboard and set to take off the day before you plan to leave. Rest your muscles as well as your brain. Have a hearty, but not rich, meal at least 3 hours before you board your boat. Keep fruit and crackers handy to the helm for your first nourishment on board. Most important, eat when hungry, not when you feel you *should*. Keeping a constant level of food-supplied energy and blood sugar is important for continuing physical and mental effectiveness.

Don't drink alcohol. Don't drink carbonated beverages. Don't eat greasy or heavily sugared foods. Not initially, at any rate. Try to eat a lot of roughage—greens, lettuce, bran and such. The change of environment and habit is likely to cause constipation, which will not only cause discomfort but also add to the fatigue problem. Get your sea legs before plunging into that pot of five-alarm chili. Moderation is the rule. Of course, there are always exceptions but, by and large, what you eat

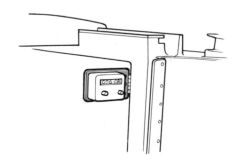

One way for a singlehander to keep abreast of his depth is to mount the sounder on a bracket that swings out and locks in the companionway. It can thus be used at the chart table and at the helm with equal ease and only a single installation.

will have a great effect on your reactions, alertness and general ability to stay awake.

Excessive amounts of coffee will *not* keep you alert. It may keep you up, but the tension it produces, added to your existing anxiety over the impending voyage, will probably cause rushed actions, erratic behavior and ill-considered judgments.

Likewise, no drugs of any kind (unless necessary for health maintenance) should be taken before or during sailing. Barbiturates and amphetamines are bad enough on land. Alone at sea, you are literally taking your life into your hands by disrupting an already ajar system and putting undue strain on your heart. Barbiturates and amphetamines impair ability to make rational decisions. The same goes for marijuana and cocaine or other narcotics. You may feel increased sensitivity and heightened perceptions, but it just ain't so. I know of one crew member, stoned on grass, who conned a 39-footer (11.8 meters) into Vineyard Haven under full sail. She claims that her one reaction afterward was overwhelming terror. And the boat and crew (all equally done in) were an absolute menace to the many other boats maneuvering in the harbor. Unless you want to take the chance of killing yourself or someone else, stay off anything that might alter your normal consciousness.

Underway, the greatest threat to staying awake is standing the helm. Sure, it's fun and exciting to steer your ship through wind and waves. It is also tiring, something like driving a car for 10 hours. If you have fitted self-steering or can rig a sheet-to-tiller rig, use it whenever you're not in congested waters. On most points of sail—depending on your boat—such an arrangement will steer a truer course than you can. By not expending the energy needed to concentrate, you'll manage to stay far more alert and will be better able to protect yourself from the elements.

Cold, wet: *tired*. The converse is true. Warm, dry: *alert*. How do you best stay that way? Most experts agree on two dressing procedures: first, wear layers of relatively light clothing: second, wear natural fibers, particularly cotton and wool. Also, fitting a

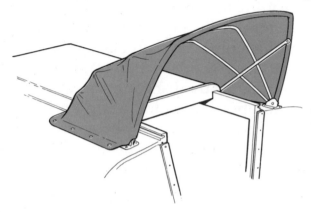

Pram hoods over the companionway or surrounding the entire forward end of the cockpit provide a dry and warm place when going to windward and protection for the cabin sole underneath; they fold out of the way when needed. The addition of clear plastic windows make watch-standing easier.

protective dodger will help, especially when beating.

Even in hot sunny weather, it's a good idea to wear loose-fitting shirts and pants. Prolonged exposure to the sun's rays produces not only a bad burn but also drowsiness, thirst and general lassitude. Cotton is best. It is soft, light and porous. Perspiration will evaporate faster than with any synthetics, leaving you cooler and more refreshed.

When it starts to get cold, and especially at night, it's time to cover up. Start with cotton underwear and a cotton flannel shirt, topped with a wool sweater. Wool is a remarkable substance; even wet it functions to retain body heat. I prefer baggy corduroys below the belt. Jeans are tough, sure, but they are tight and can bind. You are going to have to move around the deck, and you might as well be able to do it with freedom. Full-cut

Foul-weather gear with integral harness and flotation are becoming more and more popular. Certainly this makes getting dressed a far simpler process than separate devices, as well as encouraging the sailor to use a harness at all times.

corduroy trousers fit the bill. If it gets colder still, add foul weather gear, chest-high pants first. Sitting on a cold deck will make you lose more body heat from your rump than you lose from uncovered shoulders.

Whether your foul weather jacket is hooded or not is a matter of personal preference. Some sailors prefer a sou'wester. I like the hood, with a battered old tennis hat underneath or, in cold weather, a wool watch cap. Feet and hands, along with the head, are the points of greatest body heat loss. A light pair of cotton socks with wool ones over them and a good pair of large deck boots complete this fashionable outfit.

The thing to remember is to be comfortable . . . and cautious. If a storm is impending, dress beforehand. It's no use trying to get into oilies when your clothes are wet.

Assuming you're warm, dry and well fed, what else can you do to stay fresh? Learn to pace yourself. For example, in going forward to change a headsail, don't rush around, tripping over things, running back and forth between cockpit and foredeck. *Before* you go forward, take stock of the situation. What will you need? Sail bag, new sail, knife, sail ties, safety harness (if it's nighttime, you should have this on anyway). Organize all these on and about your person, clip on the harness and proceed *slowly* along the weather deck.

Okay, you've arrived at the bow. Tie the new sail bag to the pulpit and hank the new headsail onto the forestay below the still-drawing sail. Now, depending on your set-up, you've got choices. This is one reason I prefer the halyards to terminate at the mast, not the cockpit. You have only half the distance to go. Move back to the mast, slack off the jib halyard and go forward to haul down the jib. You could let the boat luff slightly during this process, since there's no one to steer things aft. Bag the jib before you do anything else, and secure it to the rail. Attach the sheets to the new sail, then the halyard. Taking the old sail with you (or stuffing it down the forehatch), move back to the mast and haul up the new sail. Go back to the cockpit, put the boat on course and trim. It's done.

Another possibility is to heave to for this task, but certain requirements must be met by both boat and rig for this to work. See the heavy weather section for details.

Try to pace yourself with everything. The best way, probably, is to draw up a series of activity plans. For each task—sail changing, anchoring, cooking, tacking and so on—sit down and actually work out exactly what you plan to do, in what order, under varying conditions.

It demands method and patience to make up list after list, step by step. You'll learn a lot in the process, too. One, that you know more than you think you do. Two, that you can probably streamline and better organize some of your activities. And that could mean greater efficiency at sea, less strain and less fatigue, not to mention greatly reduced anxiety.

Ship Management

Under the heading of ship's management comes everything involved with keeping the ship and you shipshape. Included are a number of items usually left to the crew and mate. You have two choices: learn or don't learn. Eat cans of stew and find cookie crumbs at the bottom of your sleeping bag, your ropes in Gordian knots and your socks with gaping holes. Or, you can see to it that both captain and vessel are kept Bristol fashion.

The practical advantages of keeping things in order are simple: you can find what you want when you need it, plan your store replenishment accordingly and save time and money. Psychologically, you will find yourself better organized, less subject to fatigue and in better spirits.

If an army crawls on its stomach, a sailor can be said to haul ropes on his. Since you are going to be alone, you might as well learn something about eating and stewardship. A case of hash, a loaf of bread and a jar of instant coffee do not make for good nutrition or good eating. I covered some of the precepts of nutrition on the water in the chapter on fatigue. Following are some ideas that may make things easier and certainly tastier for the novice sea cook.

This is no place for a collection of dubious

recipes. Loads of cruising cookbooks exist, though the reason escapes me. They all seem to reflect the notion that two cans and a dash of ketchup equals "gourmet" paradise.

First, learn to use your stove. Second, equip it with really sturdy pot clamps. Third, get one extra-heavy pot with a tightly fitting lid and parallel sides, and 6 inches or so in depth. You're set. Obviously, what you eat depends on your culinary skills, habits and appetite. But there is no reason to subsist on Spam and saltines.

Just like everything else, the key to good food aboard is planning. If you intend to cruise for a week, stock up for that time with *fresh* food. Eggs, vegetables, fruit, meat, all will keep for at least that long. Only the meat needs refrigeration. And with country-cured hams and bacon you can get by with hanging them from a carlin, covered in cheesecloth. Cheese is a great standby, as are dried fruits and nuts. I have a passion for chocolate bars, pumpernickel bread and stuffed grape leaves. None of these needs refrigeration and each supplies something valuable in the way of nutrients.

Stow everything with care, even in the icebox. Tossing about will ruin the best produce in no time at all. The deep sink I've mentioned will hold anything better than the highest fiddles, especially mugs of hot liquids.

Whatever you plan, try to eat when you are hungry. Three meals per day are great if you live that way at home. Personally, I find my energy level remains much higher if I eat when my stomach, not my habits, tells me to. Keep a thermos of hot water (filled after morning coffee) to supply you throughout the sail with instant soups, cocoa or other hot drinks.

A Mini-Galley or Sea-Swing stove is perfect for quick snacks. Also, don't leave dirty dishes lying around. Keep things clean and neat. In heavy weather you'll come to appreciate your housekeeping foresight. In the same vein, try not to stow cardboard boxes anywhere without wrapping them first in plastic bags. I remember one morning, on a friend's boat, opening a locker to find a mass of cornflakes treading water. Not the way I wanted to start the day.

Unless you have open water and gentle breezes ahead—very rarely do such conditions exist—plan on one-pot meals. You would be surprised at the enormous variety you can concoct. A few examples:

Stew: oil, onions, potatoes, meat or poultry, broth or juice or wine, spices. Brown chopped onions in oil, then add chunks of meat and brown. Next add liquid and cut-up potatoes and spice as you like (salt, pepper, herbs, curry, vinegar, etc., but not all at once, please). Cover and simmer until all are tender.

Hot cereals: in bad weather a godsend. Prepare oatmeal, cornmeal, whatever, as per package. Add chunks of ham, sausage (precooked) or corned beef, with lots of fresh pepper and butter.

Pasta: add about a third of a pound of pasta to salted, rapidly boiling water. Cook al dente (still firm). Drain and add oil or melt butter in the same pot. Add shrimp, cooked chicken or meat, plenty of grated Parmesan and a bit of garlic. Eat with a salad and some wine.

Toasted sandwiches: ham, cheese, tomato, onion, between two slices of any kind of bread. Fry, pressing down with a spatula until the bread is browned and the cheese melts.

Simple choucroute garnie: heat sauerkraut with sausages, ham, white wine and peppercorns. Eat with white wine and plenty of bread.

As seen from the above, ingredients can be simple and preparation will take less than half an hour, although cooking time will vary with the stove, pot thickness, and so on. With a touch of imagination, literally hundreds of nourishing, good tasting meals can be prepared with little fuss. Ernest K. Gann, the author and sailor, lives on tinned Dinty Moore Stew. Let that be his problem. Eat well instead.

Once you're well fed, you will have the energy to keep everything else well functioning. Four areas demand general and constant attention: head, cabin, engine room and deck. We might as well start with the sacred head.

In certain areas, you must by law conform to the government regulations concerning overboard discharge of human waste. Basically, you may use a holding tank system, have a macerator/chlorinator type head or use a portable head. This applies to all permanently installed toilets in any boat intidal water. In inland bodies of water, regulations permit no dumping whatsoever.

With the exception of portable heads, these systems are expensive, consume power and, in the case of holding tanks, use up one hell of a lot of space. You know my other solution: the bucket. It is not permanently mounted. Therefore, it can be used with abandon. One-third filled with seawater, and dumped overboard after each use, the bucket remains sweet and can be stowed anywhere. Cedar used to be the preferred material, but such devices are now costly. Plastic is not to be encouraged. It holds odors and, when

The cedar bucket. Though not exactly a technological marvel, it still can be one of the most useful pieces of equipment aboard. In the approved manner, always fill one-third full with seawater prior to use and always empty to leeward with circumspection.

scratched, is very hard to keep sanitary. I use a stainless steel vessel of awesome beauty with a seat I cut out of plywood and varnished.

Whichever method is used, keep a supply of biodegradable toilet paper on hand. Nothing is more unpleasant than taking a head apart to unclog it. Household tissue will clog it in no time. Also keep a set of spares: gaskets, diaphragms and such stowed by the head. A splendid way to maintain sweetness and smooth operation is to squirt ordinary dishwashing detergent into the bowl once a week and pump vigorously.

Cabins are used to live in, sleep in and eat in. A place for everything and everything in its place is an old saw, but true enough, especially within the small confines of a cruising boat. Air the bedding daily and stow it. Clean the saloon table before casting off. Don't leave books, old socks and lanterns lying around settees. They will end up on the floor, soaked. Place navigational instruments in racks. A flying compass can relieve you of an ear.

In other words, behave like a sailor, not a slob. Just because you are alone is no reason to neglect what is, in actuality, good seamanship.

Engine rooms, or engine resting places, are the most neglected area of any auxiliary. They collect grease, oil, odd bolts, rusted tools and frayed wire ends. Again the rule is: Keep it clean and organized. Engine pans should be mopped regularly, stray dirt and grime wiped off the block, spares carried— plugs and ignition parts for gasoline engines, impellers for diesels. Better yet, have the engine maker make up a spare parts kit. You need tools at the ready which fit the various bolt heads and pipes sticking out all over. An engine with hand-starting capability is a great boon, especially as batteries have a way of dying when you most need them. These, by the way, should be tightly strapped into boxes, well ventilated and away from seawater (the combination can produce hydrogen gas).

Finally, the most important and most neglected area of shipkeeping—the deck. Here is where you spend most of your time, where most hazards exist, what your neighbors most see. Keep it neat. Coil lines, tie off halyards, brake the wheel or tie the tiller, use chafe gear, wipe up the peanut butter and make sure all deck fittings are tightly fastened and functioning. Cover the mainsail. Tighten the mainsheet and don't leave anything loose to blow away or be kicked overboard.

If you think about it, all the areas of ship management concern your eventual safety. The boat can go down to the gurgle of an open seacock; an engine won't start as you are heading toward a tanker, or something sharp flying off a table can incapacitate you—all are potential disasters. Care and concern in keeping things as they should be will pay off.

6. Standing Watch and Watching Out

The 1972 COLREGS (International Regulations for Avoiding Collision at Sea) are quite explicit: all ships must post a lookout at all times. That many don't and that the seas of the world are filled with wrecks should be warning enough to any sailor. If you are sailing alone, you can duck below for a few moments to get food, plot position and such, but your visible horizon must be clear of traffic even for that.

Some singlehanders develop a knack for sleeping an hour at a time. Some can sleep normal hours, especially in seldom traveled areas. But in coastal passages, there is little advice I can offer that will allow you to keep to the letter *and* spirit of the law as well as permit you to sleep.

Modern boats do not heave to well, so you will either have to stay awake or else anchor for the night. The risks are too great to suggest anything else. I have seen fully crewed boats run down by a long tow in broad daylight on a clear day. Inattention was the cause. When you're alone, the chances of being hit are multiplied so many times that no bookmaker would place odds.

Assuming you plan to stay awake for the duration of the passage, what can be done to make sure you don't get run down? Rick Butler, a U.S. Navy Commander and very experienced big ship driver, suggests the

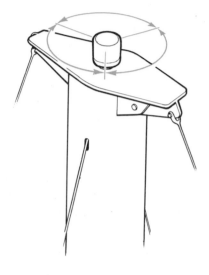

Regulation masthead tri-color lights are far more visible than traditional pulpit-mounted ones, which are liable not to be seen through the waves. Remember to replace the bulb at the start of each season. The last thing you want to do is clamber up the mast on a rainy night.

In an emergency, when the electrics go by the board, a windproof kerosene/paraffin lantern can be hoisted in the rigging to warn off other ships. I strongly suggest you test such a lantern in real conditions before rely-ing on it. Very few so-called "windproof" lamps actually are. The best I know is the traditional pattern Davey.

following (amended and simplified by me):

1. Install a masthead-mounted strobe light.

2. See if your sails can have foil-coated headboards installed and, if you have a vane, install aluminum-covered Mylar film on the vane itself.

3. Offshore, consider tanbark colored sails. White doesn't show up well from a distance.

4. If you can't do the masthead strobe number, use a man-overboard strobe for signaling your position.

5. Have a big spotlight aboard. Aim at the oncoming ship, not your sails.

6. As soon as you can guess his course, steer away from his track. Don't wait! Modern ships move a sea mile every two minutes.

7. Never use flares to identify yourself. They may attract would-be rescuers who could run you down.

8. Most standard pleasure boat navigation lights cannot be seen readily. Get big ones and mount them as high as possible. The ideal solution is a tricolor masthead light combined with your strobe. Red and green

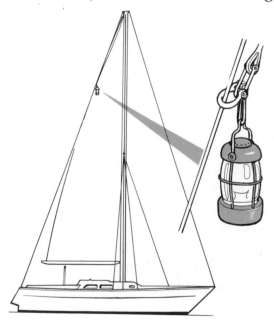

running lights should be mounted on the pulpit, not the deckhouse or cabin. Sails will obscure them.

9. Always assume the ship will NOT see you.

10. Forget the fact that ships are supposed to stay in regular lanes. On the open oceans, ships today use Optimum Track Ship's Routing (OTSR) and stray far from those pilot chart tracks.

Also, the old rule "sail has the right of way" can be thoroughly discounted. If you are aboard a 300-foot-long (90 meters) full-rigged ship, maybe. Otherwise, run like hell!

The above may keep ships from running you down, but they won't help you avoid stationary obstructions that happen to be in your path. Currents, wind shifts and compass deviation can have a disastrous effect on your course. You must know where you are, certainly a function of the most basic navigation. Nevertheless, experienced sailors have found themselves thrown 30 or more miles (48 km) off course by adverse currents, beer cans next to the binnacle (and batteries in flashlights too) or wind shifts in the middle of the night.

A safe rule to follow is that when you're nearer to shore than 50 miles (80 km), stay awake, and stay in the cockpit or wheelhouse. Further out—except in port approaches such as Boston Harbor, San Francisco Bay, anything along the southern coast of England, off Durban, and so on—a certain amount of sleep is a safer bet, but you can never be sure when a ship will come over the horizon and "discover" you.

Although I have not used them, off-course alarms and radar detectors may help. Off-course alarms are activated by a sensor compass, set to ring when a course is surpassed either side by 10 degrees or so. They have been used with varying degrees of success. They are expensive and, like all electronics, they are subject to corrosion and malfunction. But they are certainly worth a try if you sail offshore with any regularity.

Radar detectors are simpler and cheaper. An alarm is activated when a signal is received from big ship radar. Since signals vary, set the alarm for several ranges, say 8, 16, 32 and 48 miles (13, 26, 52 and 65 km). A minimum range of 8 miles will allow you to take evasive action and maneuver away from the potential dangers.

Nevertheless, none of these devices or visual aids will substitute for a properly kept watch, scanning the horizon—a full 360 degrees—every 10 minutes at the absolute minimum. Singlehanding is best for a short coastal passage or a long haul. The intermediate voyages of two to four or five days are potentially the most dangerous and demand the greatest care and planning of all.

7. Safety

Safety considerations for the singlehander are not much different from those aboard the fully crewed yacht. The differences lie mainly in the deployment of materials and devices, and in the added precautions that must be taken. The primary consideration, especially if the boat is fitted with a self-steering device, is staying in the boat.

To that end, lifelines should be installed. Stanchions must be at least 24 inches (61 cm) high, preferably 27 (69 cm) or even 30 (76 cm). Lifelines are effective only if you don't pitch over them or under them. Double or triple lines are called for in any serious passage undertaken alone. Made of wire, coated or not, or of Dacron rope (less painful and cheaper), they should be fitted with toggles or end fittings that allow adjustment and fatigue-free movement. Gates are a problem. Although they are convenient, they are the weak link in the chain, since a number of pelican hooks on the market are cheaply manufactured in the Far East. If you are agile enough to singlehand, you can probably do with clambering over lifelines. Pulpit and stern rail must be strong and also high. Too often they are designed to keep sails and cushions from going over, and not 200 pounds (90 km) of accelerating humanity. The force of a body thrown across a deck is awesome and capable of ripping out rails.

Second, you must always wear a safety harness at night and in anything over a force

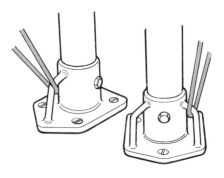

Stanchion bases must be through-bolted and have high enough side walls to securely support the uprights. Also, there should be set screws to secure the stanchions, as well as bails to attach blocks, lines, fenders and such.

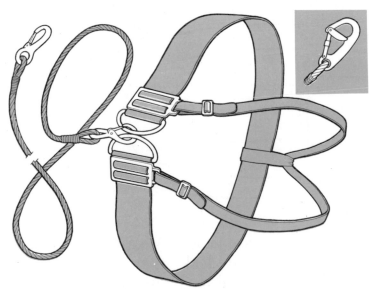

A reliable safety harness will be to approved government standards, with nonmagnetic metal parts, triple-stiched webbing and a proof-tested and nontripping safety hook, such as this one by Gibb.

4—5. I know singlehanders who don't, and I hope their families survive their grief and enjoy the insurance. Be confident, but don't be foolish! The type of harness to wear is a touchy question. In Great Britain, a standard exists for "proofed" harnesses. In America, you have to trust the maker. Try for something with 2-inch (5 cm) webbing, welded, triple-stitched, with stainless steel rings and fasteners. The line should be braided Dacron or nylon (which absorbs more of a sudden shock) at least 7/16 inch (1.2 cm) in diameter. It should be spliced to the harness ring, terminating in an eyespliced snap hook of some sort. I say "some sort" because the most tested hooks are probably the type used by mountain climbers. Some marine hooks have been known to bend, twist, jam and fail. Not a pleasant thought. Some harness lines are equipped with two hooks on one line. I prefer two separate lines, each about 6 feet (1.5 meters) long. This arrangement allows you to hook up the second before you unhook the first.

What do you attach your harness lines to? The best arrangement I know of, and the one

For a safety harness to be effective, jacklines as shown here are needed. They should be made up of plastic-coated wire securely attached—Norseman, Sta-Lok or Talurit with thimble ends—and the deck pads need be through-bolted with backing pads. Ideally they should run as close to the centerline as possible. Hooking on to lifelines instead of jacklines can be guaranteed to throw you overboard, because they are so far outboard.

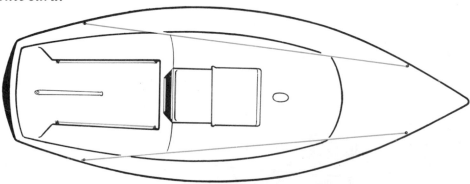

I use, is two wire jacklines run from the cockpit to the foredeck, as close to the centerline as possible. These must be attached

at either end to strong, through-bolted pad eyes by either Norseman terminals or swaged-end fittings. Toggles are a good idea to lessen twisting strains.

Another good idea is stainless-steel handrails on either side and around the companionway hatch. These will usually allow you to clip on and move either aft to the helm or forward to the mast. The handrails must be through-bolted.

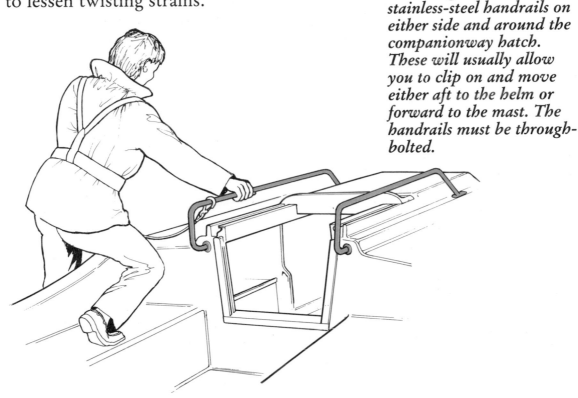

Be sure to hook on before you come out of the companionway. Too often, sailors have been swept out of a cockpit. Try not to clip onto the lifelines. They will tend to act as a fulcrum to flip you overboard, whereas a centerline connection makes the lifelines into a body stop. Also, the jacklines allow for unimpeded movement fore and aft.

A float coat is a good idea at night, and there are some oilskin jackets fitted with internal harnesses, particularly those made by Henri-Lloyd and Atlantis. I find life jackets extremely constricting, but you ought to keep one handy. If the Coast Guard ever gets around to approving the inflating type, very popular in Europe, people may be more willing to wear them.

The actual surface of the deck is usually overlooked. Most of the molded-in nonskid types are pathetic, except for collecting dirt. Nonskid paint is better, and teak is best of all, if you can afford it. Be sure that angled surfaces—the fore end of the cabin top, coamings, cockpit seats—are covered. Attractiveness must play second fiddle to safety.

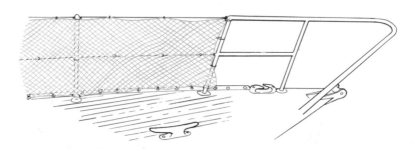

Safety netting, made of nylon expressly for the purpose, is useful to prevent small objects, sails and children from sliding overboard under the lower lifeline. It can be lashed to the upper line and a slotted toerail as shown, or the bottom can be lashed to small screweyes installed in the wood rail.

Cabin tops and deckhouses should be equipped with plenty of through-bolted handrails made of wood and unvarnished. Besides being a pain to keep up, varnished wood is slippery enough to foil the basic purpose of a handrail.

No matter what, always go forward on the weather side of the boat. In a sudden lurch you won't be thrown over. In larger boats, safety pulpits on either side of the mast can be a boon in heavy weather.

What happens if you go overboard? Assuming your harness holds, you've got to get back on board. Unless you're a professional athlete, you will *not* be able to haul yourself over the rail, especially if the boat is moving at anything over 3 knots. You have suddenly added 40 to 60 pounds (18 to 27 kilos) of water, plus the unbelievable drag of your body through the sea. Some sort of ladder is a must. For a singlehander there are really only two choices: a permanently mounted stern ladder or a quick-release

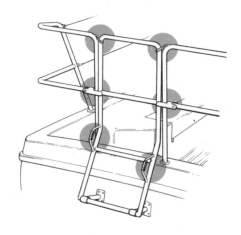

emergency boarding ladder. The stern-mounted construction can be of several varieties: reaching below the waterline, folding down (in which case, a lanyard dangling to the water to lower it should be installed) or, if your ship is fitted with a transom-hung rudder, a series of steps, starting below the waterline and bolted to the rudder blade. Quick-release ladders are usually made of PVC runged rope, rolled up, with a lanyard dangling over the side. You attach them to the deck or stern rail and pull. With luck, they'll unfold.

A trailing line is most important. Generally, the best choice is polypropylene,

Not only useful for boarding the dinghy and getting aboard from a swim, a stern-mounted boarding ladder can be the difference between life and death should a singlehander go overboard. A lanyard attached to the bottom rung and left trailing will allow someone in the water to bring the steps down to a boarding position.

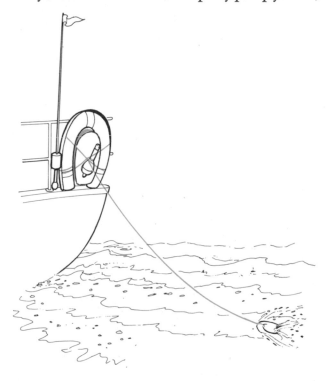

Another safety measure for the singlehander is to have the dan buoy, man-overboard pole and horseshoe attached to a trailing line ending in a small float. If you do fall overboard, you will be able to grab the float and bring all the above gear into the water while at the same time disengaging the self-steering (see page 82).

which floats, with a buoyant ring secured to the trailing end. My experience has been that one about 75 feet (22.5 meters) long is adequate. You'd be surprised how fast the boat can get ahead of you when you pitch overboard.

Richard Henderson, in his excellent book *Singlehanded Sailing*, describes a method for attaching the trailing line to the self-steering

Using a snap shackle as diagrammed here will allow a singlehander to get back to the ship should he go overboard. Tying the arrangement in with the man-overboard gear (see page 81) will allow time to rest and think in the water while remaining attached to the ship. Also, of course, the yacht will round up and/or slow down, allowing you to get back on board.

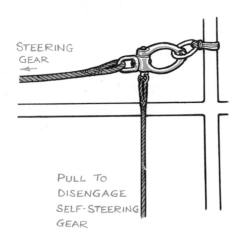

STEERING GEAR

PULL TO DISENGAGE SELF-STEERING GEAR

tiller lines by means of a snap shackle. You fall over, grab the ring and the self-steering is tripped, causing the boat to round up. A thoughtful and worthwhile idea. Even with crew aboard, this isn't a bad practice. By the time they get on deck, you might well be lost in the waves. In fact, the trip line could probably be doubled, so as to also release the horseshoe and man-overboard pole, and activate a warning light below. Anything to increase safety is prudent.

The life raft should be mounted on deck. Too often it is shoved into a locker with assorted gear piled on top—not exactly where you want it when you need it. Forward or abaft the mast is a good place in that it will allow a fairly clear platform to launch the raft. Remember always to attach the tether to a strongpoint on deck.

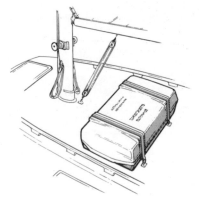

For any boat going offshore, an inspected life raft is a must. They are expensive to buy and expensive to service, but they can be your only lifesaving device if the boat has the temerity to sink under you. Buy the best and rig it so it will float clear of the deck or cockpit when it must. Don't put it in a locker. A waterproof duffel filled with extras not included in the raft survival pack should be lashed near the companionway. This can be packed with extra water, space blankets, food supplements, navigational tools and charts, a handbearing compass and repair materials for the raft. Don't forget writing materials and a jar of vaseline (for salt water sores). Allow a pint of water per day.

It's a good idea to keep a waterproof bag of emergency supplies just inside the companionway. This way, you'll have additional food and water, as well as any other navigational gear and survival equipment not included in the standard raft pack, should you abandon ship.

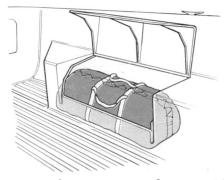

When you buy your raft, consider double floors and a ballast chamber. The Fastnet disaster showed that, in certain conditions, standard rafts are less than life saving. Givens, Avon, Beaufort, Dunlop, RDF, Surviva and Zodiac all make good rafts. Just remember, you get only what you pay for. One afterthought: the raft will be better off (and you will too) if it's a cannister pack. Valises, though handier to stow, may permit corrosion of the inflating valves through exposure.

Parachute flares should be part and parcel of the raft or boat. Very or flare pistols can corrode, so the self-contained, high power

Valise-packed rafts should not be left in the open, as moisture can seep in and corrode or jam the inflation valves. A cockpit locker devoted solely to the raft is a good idea in this case. When underway, it must never be locked.

Always throw the liferaft clear of the yacht to inflate. If it is inflated on board, it may get caught in the rigging and could go down with the ship!

Once the raft is clear, inflate it by giving the lanyard a smart pull. If the raft does not inflate, then pull one end aboard and attempt to inflate it manually.

flares are probably the best. These are not cheap but they are effective and have a three-year shelf life. Check the date. At least half a dozen is mandatory for both boat and raft, so keep the checkbook handy. And learn how to use them beforehand. Reading directions in the dark aboard a sinking ship is not easy.

A permanently mounted radar reflector is a necessary safety measure. Masthead reflectors are a nuisance, although they are the most effective. I carry mine wired to the backstay, 20 feet (6 meters) up.

Providing access to the masthead is vital, and mast steps are to be recommended on anything over 30 feet (9 meters). The alternative is a bosun's chair, the best of which are made of cloth, with safety straps. Be sure to rig a line that runs from the chair around the mast and is secured again to the chair. Keeps you from flying.

Bilge pumps are as important as engines. Have two manual pumps, one operable from the cockpit through a watertight gland, one inside the cabin. Despite the standard, I feel both should be capable of disposing of at least 25 gallons (95 litres) per minute. Anything less is for pumping out rainwater. Henderson, Whale and Edson make the best.

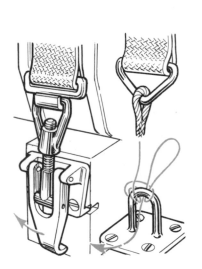

The raft must be kept secure on the deck yet at the same time be capable of being freed with ease. Either of these methods is satisfactory: a patent adjustable catch or a padeye with light lashings that can be cut with a knife.

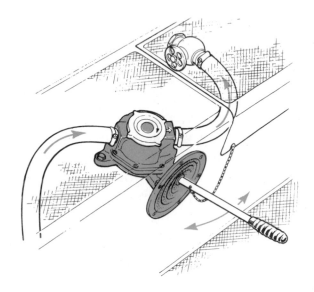

Bilge pumps must be handy to the helm. They should also be usable with all lockers closed. Be sure that exit ports are-fitted with seacocks or gate valves and that these are easy to reach.

The above are just the basics. Unfortunately, the rest can be learned only through experience, plus a lot of talking and listening to *sailors*, not dockside kibitzers.

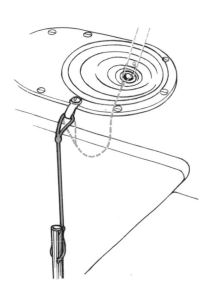

Like winch handles, pump handles have a tendency to get lost overboard. Drill a small hole in the shaft of the handle and attach it with light line to a padeye or fitting on deck close enough to the pump so it can be used with ease.

8. Heavy Weather

Sooner or later you will be caught out in heavy weather—a passing squall or full gale offshore. You must be prepared physically, mentally and technically. You may think a squall is bad news, but wait until you have a storm at sea, with horizontal rain, 30- to 50-knot winds, and 20- or 30-foot (6 or 9 meters) seas. Your experiences with small storms can be, and must be, training for handling your ship with greater assurance and courage when you are faced with serious and dangerous weather conditions.

The old adage that to windward a boat can stand more than a man, and offwind a man can stand more than a boat, has great truth in it. Fighting a gale is exhausting, wet, stomach-churning work. Unless you must claw off a lee shore, run for it. Usually boat speed is so great downwind, even with no sail, that sometimes it is necessary to slow down just to survive. Survival is a matter of keeping boat and sea in rhythm. This is much easier in open waters offshore than in proximity to the continental shelf. Monster rollers can be "danced with" better than the steep coastal chop of breakers near shore.

How you go about "dancing" is another matter, depending on hull shape, rig, lateral plane, displacement and a number of other factors. But you must move with the sea, not against it. Its power is very real and very frightening. I have seen, on a trans-Atlantic crossing, a force 10 turn stainless steel stanchions and a Hasler vane gear into spaghetti. A 20-foot (6 meters) wave coming down on the deck, backed by several hundred miles or kilometers of sweep and the acceleration of wind and gravity, can break a Lloyds-approved boat in half. And a freak wave can do worse—witness the tragedy that befell *Morning Cloud*.

Back to our original assumption that you own a fin-keel boat of moderately light displacement, with a sloop or cutter rig, low wetted surface, wide beam and not much under water. Under such circumstances, experience seems to indicate that running at high speed may well be the best answer in storm conditions. Eric Tabarly has used such tactics in the southern oceans and has survived. However, much would seem to depend on wave patterns and steepness. A boat with the above characteristics would be naturally buoyant, and would tend to ride the waves. But with the new designs that favor fine bows and a broad, flat stern, the chances of pitchpoling in particularly steep seas is something to think about before running hard.

It may well be wise to consider streaming warps aft. Lengths of your heaviest line (which for most sailors these days ain't

While running in severe conditions it will be necessary to slow the ship considerably. Trailing a bight of heavy line from the quarters may be highly effective, especially as the length can be adjusted to coincide with the rhythm of the seas.

much) should be belayed to the strongest fittings aft, and let overboard. Two 100-foot (30 meters) long ¾-inch (2 cm) lines will have a remarkable effect, slowing a 30-footer (9 meters) by as much as two or three knots.

Heaving-to is not just a heavy weather tactic. It is especially useful for singlehanders who need a respite in bad weather or want to prepare a meal and cannot otherwise leave the helm. Modern fin-keel yachts will not always heave-to with ease. Experiments with sail area and set may be needed.

Heaving to, the technique by which you back the jib or reefed main and lash the tiller to leeward, works only with a ship of reasonable lateral plane. It would be very difficult to get any modern fin-keeler to heave to. More likely it would broach. A full-keeled or, I should say, long-keeled boat will do a much better job of it. The tiller (or wheel) must be lashed to a greater or lesser degree, which can be determined only by your experience with a particular boat. When all is set, the boat should forereach at a couple of knots. Traditionally, in the days when sail had the right of way, you could carry out this maneuver on the starboard tack (which is why, traditionally, the galley was to port). In our day, when no one pays the slightest attention to sailors except other sailors, heaving to is not practiced much.

Certainly, in confined waters or on coastal passages it is not a tactic to be recommended unless some distance offshore, and not a lee shore at that. Rod Stephens has said that he thought a number of the boats in the Fastnet disaster were caught out because they hadn't great enough lateral planes to attempt heaving to. A CCA boat would have had a better chance.

Hulling, or lying a-hull, is another heavy weather favorite, but there is certainly a lot of

Lying ahull can be effective if the boat is not too deep-keeled and the windage aloft is balanced by reasonable underwater area. The idea is to keep the boat from tripping over into a roll while at the same time not being so stiff that rig or deck gear could be smashed.

confusion about the subject. Richard Henderson, in *East to the Azores*, writes an informed and thoughtful section on this.

Problems with hulling depend very much on the boat. A deep keel can cause tripping, sending you into a capsize (we are talking about extreme weather, remember). A shallow draft will probably be much more comfortable, though the leeway will be greater. In a centerboarder, the board should probably be raised, since the strains put upon hull and rigging are extreme. I find that my own boat, hulling in heavy weather, will not quite lie beam-on, but rather will point slightly upwind, causing some burying of the bows. However, as my boat is of fairly light displacement, I don't worry too much. It lifts to the seas.

The boat will take up whatever attitude it wishes on its own, and your attempts to alter that stance will probably spell disaster. A well-found and well-built modern boat will undoubtedly survive much greater abuse from the sea than one of Claude Worth's cutters, or even a boat like *Wanderer III*. Extreme heavy displacement will make for greater comfort, but I doubt that such a boat will be as safe in heavy going as a moderate or lightweight vessel. What is important in any vessel is reserve bouyancy fore and aft. Moderate overhangs with flare in the bow seem to be a wise idea. The stern shape doesn't matter at all as long as the reserve is there and the run aft is clean.

I have run off in canoe sterns, transom sterns, all of them. The only trouble I had was in a Concordia yawl—which has a very fine stern indeed—and we got pooped twice. I have never been in a survival storm (and sincerely hope never to be), but have known sailors who have. In those conditions, simply

With proper storm canvas or well-reefed sails it should be possible to beat off a lee shore in a gale. This assumes a weatherly hull and the skills to use these sail combinations successfully. Practice in moderate weather will familiarize you with the limitations of shortened canvas.

staying afloat seems to be the major concern. No one has time to worry about the aesthetics or wave-breaking efficiency of the stern. It probably wouldn't matter anyhow.

Your first concern with seas and wind on the rise will be shortening sail. Once again, this is a matter of rig. In a cutter you can drop the jib, reef the main and keep going. In a sloop, reef the main and go to smaller and smaller jibs. Two-stick rigs will usually balance with foresail and mizzen, but I question the advisability of the combination. With such a rig the strains are great, and with a triatic stay you are chancing loosing the mainmast. Better to reef the main and drop the mizzen, unless the mizzen is very small and can be used for balancing purposes.

Whatever, if you go more than a few miles or kilometers offshore, the boat must have storm sails, and you must know how to use them.

A storm jib is no problem to rig, except that it must always be properly led aft. I prefer a permanently-bent-on sheet with no hardware and screw-in deck blocks. The clew should be padded with leather or some other resilient material. The leads are important. A genoa track doesn't go far enough forward to be of any use, and it is too far outboard. Actually, a self-tending storm jib is possible with a rope traveler.

Remember to have your sailmaker install head and tack pennants of very stout wire.

A trysail is a most important bit of canvas, although very few are seen or used on the American side of the Atlantic. However, when you need it, there is no substitute. It should be roped all around and should run up its own track for lacing around the mast, perhaps the best solution for the occasional singlehander. It should not sheet to the end of the boom. After all, you may wish to lash the boom to the house. Better to lead the sheets, also permanently bent on, to the quarters. Make sure your stern cleats are really substantial. You won't have to worry about winches because you will sheet a trysail flat. It becomes essentially self-tacking.

Both storm sails deserve the consideration of the best cloth and triple stitching. You may use them only once every ten years, but they could save your life and your ship. The fact that you will rarely use them makes it all the more important that you rehearse setting and dousing both. Back to the Fastnet. The report told of many crews who couldn't set storm sails. No provision had been made for them. You try hanking a storm jib on a grooved foil headstay! Sure the Fastnet storm was a freak; so was the hurricane of 1938, and thousands of squalls, depressions, cyclones and other oddments of Mother Nature.

Storm sails must be set before the storm, especially when singlehanding. Prudence and caution are the watchwords. Even 40 square feet (3.6 square meters) of jib can batter you to utter exhaustion in 50-knot winds. Watch the weather, especially the barometer. When you have trouble sheeting in the working jib, change down. After two reefs, no main will be really effective, and the boom becomes a potential murderer. When the boat is over-canvassed with storm jib and double-reefed main, change down to trysail and jib, or trysail alone. If that's too much, survival tactics apply, and running under bare poles and/or with warps trailing may be the best lifesaver, if you have sea room.

Some points to consider in heavy weather:
• When the weather deteriorates to a point where handling ship under reduced sail becomes difficult, when the size of the seas endangers the integrity of the ship, or when progress in a safe direction becomes near impossible, you are in danger. These three criteria are not the only ones, but they can serve as a good guide to the next set of maneuvers. All are dependent on weather fronts, winds and depressions. The size and displacement of your vessel will have some bearing upon the meeting of the above conditions. Obviously a ketch of 50 feet (15 meters) LOA will be able to cope with large seas with greater assurance and safety than a power vessel of 30 feet (10 meters) LOA. Any sound vessel, however, can undertake precautionary maneuvers to allow more or less equitable coping with bad conditions.
• When the wind pipes up, the first thing to do is to reduce sail. However, balance is equally important, especially when reaching or beating to windward. The larger vessel's ability to hold a course longer in a rising wind than a small boat can is due to displacement and sail-

carrying ability. The key is to keep green water from coming aboard. When the weather is truly nasty, reduction of speed is invariably the best seamanlike judgment.

● Everything on deck *and* below must be secured in heavy weather. Sails, anchors, lines, life raft, you must be attached to the boat in a manner that precludes loss overboard. You must be in a life harness.

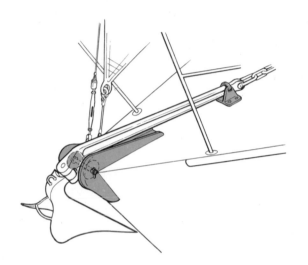

Securing the main anchor at the ready is vital, especially with onshore winds and a shelving bottom. A CQR in a bow roller with a drophead pin and a chock for the shank is certainly the most convenient way of going about it.

Anchors should be given double lashings with heavy line . . . a loose object of such shape and weight can easily hole a hull, given the opportunity. Below decks, batteries have to be tied down, locker doors strong and secure—no friction or magnetic catches—books fiddled or lashed in place, stove gimbals closed, etc. Even floorboards should be able to be fastened, perhaps with button catches. In a knockdown, you will have a mess below, but any heavy object or glass or sharp implement can cause major injuries or even death. Try to avoid the worst. At the beginning of the season, it's even a good idea to tighten the engine bed fastenings. There have been cases of engines tearing

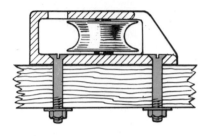

All deck fittings must be through-bolted with backing plates. The strains imposed in heavy-weather sailing can otherwise rip even the most robust hardware from its position.

loose from their mountings and causing boats to founder. Be sure to secure all hatches, ventilators, hatchboards and seacocks.

● Safety harnesses are *de rigeur* at night and in anything over a force 5. They ought to be government standard with two lanyards with proofed hooks/snaps. Deck attachment points must be through-bolted. Lacking such, or in emergencies, you can lash yourself to binnacle or tracks.

● As the weather deteriorates you need to be fresh, alert, sensitive. You must keep a watch to windward for approaching waves, and must be alert to the need for sudden maneuvers. Keep as protected, warm and dry as possible.

● Sailing to windward demands not only a good eye. The necessity of pacing the boat to the height of the waves is vital. The helm should luff slightly as she comes down the face of a wave, slowing the boat and allowing the bow to rise to the oncoming crest. Otherwise there is a good chance of burying the bow and causing loss and damage to the deck gear. The boat should have minimum steerage when approaching the crest of the next wave, as the speed generated surfing down the back of the wave will usually be sufficient to ascend the next one. The maneuver is one of weaving, increasing and decreasing speed offwind and upwind so as to keep the boat moving with a reasonable motion and as little threat to ship and crew as possible.

● In really heavy weather, sailing in a beam sea can be courting disaster. Cresting waves can fill cockpits, cause knockdowns, or stave in a deckhouse. In less momentous seas, a tendency to broach or a difficulty in steering will probably be experienced.

Either shorten sail or head off with the wind on the quarter.

• Running can be an exhilarating experience. However, when seas build to a point where steering becomes difficult, extreme care will be needed at the helm to avoid a broach. In gale or storm conditions, don't play racer and try to carry spinnakers. Rather, reduce sail to a point where the boat is moving at optimum speed, neither in danger of surfing so fast as to be falling off wave tops nor so slow as to lose steerage way. In midocean monster storms, the need will almost always be to slow the boat down.

• To reduce speed in severe running conditions, several methods are available. With most modern sailing vessels, the sea anchor is to be avoided. The strains it puts on the ship are greater than the advantages, and there is usually not enough forefoot to the vessel for it to keep the bow to the wind. Trailing warps does work. However, they must be many and attached so as to distribute the strains around the ship. Occasionally, anchors can be trailed from warps or bundles of chain. However, be sure to rig tripping devices or you may never get the goods aboard again. Ideally, you will let them out as needed. This does assume, however, that several hundred feet or meters of heavy line are aboard. Oil spread overboard either from the toilet or by means of a can or bag can be effective, but very few modern yachts ever have the capacity or availability of product to deploy effectively this method of calming the seas. Also, such tactics demand a very slow moving or still vessel. It may be most effective when lying a-hull or hove to.

• Lying a-hull is when all sail is stowed,

tiller is lashed, and the ship left to look after herself. This can be a perfectly sound tactic, providing sea room exists for leeward drift and some forward motion due to the area presented by rigging, spars and hull and tophamper. Some experiences have suggested that a shallow-hulled craft will be safer at this maneuver than a deep-draft one, as the deep keel can cause a tripping effect in certain sized seas, possibly causing a knockdown or rollover. It is also a good tactic for the single-hander in a small boat.

• Heaving to is perhaps the simplest method of slowing a boat down and giving yourself rest in heavy going. The only maneuver required is to tack, leaving the headsail as is. Ease the main and lash the tiller to leeward. Then, depending upon adjustments of mainsheet and tiller, the boat will forereach slowly—dependent to some degree upon tophamper, sail area, keel depth, etc. The headsail should be brought in tightly before heaving to and, in heavier conditions, the main might well be dropped and secured. Of course, leeway will be made, and heaving to should not be attempted on a lee shore unless for a short time and with little sail and a deep-draft hull. Even then, adjustments must be made to allow for as little leeway as possible, perhaps by trimming the main to allow stronger forereaching. Chafe is always a problem when hove to; the practice is better with a working jib or storm jib than with a genoa or lapper. In very heavy going, some chafe protection around the sheet where it crosses the shrouds will not be amiss. The old saw about heaving to on the starboard tack has little relevance today, as most commercial shipping will not alter course, even if they see you. A controversial point, to say the least.

- In "survival conditions"—force 10 and upward—the only possible point of sail will be running. In fact, because of the strength of the wind and the severity and height of the seas, you will run no matter what. In such circumstances, it is best to rid the decks of any and all impedimenta that may be carried away or hamper such working of the deck as is possible. As mentioned before, oil or trailing warps is probably the best tactic. The warps should be streamed one at a time until the speed of the ship is lowered to the point where control is possible and following seas present the least threat. Extraordinary concentration at the helm is necessary and watches should be kept short if possible. If the lines trailed are in a bight and long enough to coincide with the seas aft, the bight may well serve to inhibit crests and smooth the attacking demons. In any storm or "ultimate" seas, stay with the boat unless it is truly foundering. Life rafts, as shown by the Fastnet disaster in 1979, are too easily flipped, drift away or cannot be entered with any degree of safety. Even with improvements—ballast pockets, drogues, heavy tether lines— chances are that you will be safer in the mother ship so long as she remains tight. Whatever, be prepared!

9.
Emergencies

For a singlehander, nothing is more terrifying than going overboard. No man-overboard drills practiced with crew mean a damn thing. Prior preparation and practice is vital to saving one's life. Period. No exceptions.

Just before the beginning of the first OSTAR, Blondie Hasler was asked what would happen if someone fell overboard. Legend has it he replied, "I hope he would have the grace to drown like a gentleman." It is certainly one possibility, though not one I would like to consider.

Better to consider another activity plan, a what-would-I-do-if-it-actually-happened scenario. The obvious is to avoid going over the side at all costs. Wear a safety harness at night and whenever you leave the cockpit, even in moderate weather. Only one slip of the foot is necessary for disaster to strike. Safety harnesses are not comfortable. They are clumsy and awkward and dig in at all the wrong places. Some, however, work. In England, you can buy one with a *Kitemark*, which guarantees its having been tested according to British Government standards, which are very stringent.

Make sure that lifelines are high enough and that stanchions are really through-bolted. Most boats come with single lifelines. Get double ones. It is very easy to slip beneath one line. If the top lifeline is encased in vinyl, it will be easier to grab, but clear plastic allows you to inspect the wire. High enough?

At least 24 inches (61 cm), preferably 27 (69 cm) and ideally 30 (76 cm). I have seen a few ocean voyaging boats with 30-inch-high (76 cm) *triple* lines. That's careful planning.

Gates in lifelines are nice if you wear a kilt, but the weak link is the pelican hook closure. Gibb and Johnson both make safety catch hooks that I highly recommend and, should you decide on gates, be sure to install braces for the stanchions either side.

Wire lifelines running down the centerline have been discussed in the safety chapter, as have proper handrails.

Assuming you've done everything possible to stay in the boat, what happens if you still flip over the side? You've got to get back on board. Unless you're hand steering, the boat will continue on its merry way, not having any response to weather helm.

Precautions to take for getting back aboard include:

First, trail a polypropylene line—50 to 100 feet (15 to 30 meters) long—from a stern cleat. Tie a small buoy to the trailing end. Poly lines float, and if you can find one in a Day-Glo color, all the better.

Second, mount a ladder that is reachable from the stern. It can be a drop-down stainless steel one, or a rope with a release line. Assuming the boat is whizzing along at 5 or 6 knots, you will, with all your clothes, have a very difficult time hauling yourself to the stern. You will be exhausted. Even climbing a ladder will be a Herculean feat. If you happen to have a boat fitted with a transom-hung rudder, steps can be attached to the rudder blade. No matter what type of ladder you use, make sure the bottom two rungs sink well below the surface. Weight them if necessary with a small lead pig.

If you are equipped with self-steering,

arrange a trailing line that will trip the steering gear. Another solution must be arrived at for vanes that do not employ tiller lines, especially those with separate, servo-assisted rudders.

Provided you are able to get back on board, you will be exhausted, cold, very wet and possibly on the verge of shock. If you're in clear waters, get below instantly, get out of *all* your clothes, put on the heaviest, warmest things you've got, especially for your feet and hands, and get something warm into your stomach. Don't drink alcohol! But soup, tea or cocoa will warm you with no after effects. Drink slowly and give your body time to build up its temperature again. Even 10 minutes in temperate water (about 65°F or 18°C) can lower your body temperature considerably, especially as you are losing even more body heat in your attempts to get back aboard.

Another area of concern to the singlehander is injury or illness. I remember sailing dead downwind for 11 hours with a high fever, trying to reach port, where I could get aid and assistance. I knew I had the flu, but I had no desire to fight it out alone in an isolated cove. During those 11 hours, I fell asleep three times. I was foolish and did something that could have ended tragically. The boat was well stocked, I knew what was wrong with me and I should have stayed put for a couple of days. But I had to get back to the office.

The moral of the story is: be prepared. Have a good medical kit, learn how to administer basic first aid to yourself and think about how you will manage if you are *slightly* disabled. If you develop serious illness, or sustain serious bodily injury, obviously you must seek help by any means, and the quickest means possible. But if the damage is slight, you alone must decide if you are able to continue safely to your destination.

Your first aid kit is of vital importance. It is your only line of defense. Don't assume for a moment that the little plastic boxes with red crosses on top that you buy from your chandlery are adequate for more than cuts and scrapes. True, you will suffer from cuts and scrapes, occasional pulled muscles and sunburn most often. Nevertheless, it is essential that you buy a good marine first aid book. Go over their suggested drug and medical supply lists with your own doctor, taking into account any particular physical and emotional problems you may suffer from. Then, armed with real information and a few prescriptions, visit your local druggist and place your purchases in a watertight plastic or metal container within easy reach of your companionway.

You will notice the mention of emotional problems. Sailors are supposed to be a hearty, rough bunch. However, they are also human. Fear, trepidation and insecurity are but a few of the problems common to many, and especially to singlehanders. Confidence doesn't come until you've done it. Your emotional state is 100 percent as important to successful passagemaking as is your physical well-being. Witness the tragic end to Donald Crowhearst, the round-the-world racer who tried to fool the world and ended up committing suicide.

The advice in the chapter on fatigue is good preventive medicine. Cuts and such deserve a Band-Aid. Headaches, two aspirin. But a broken arm, a head injury, a large gash or anything infected—not to mention symptoms of severe internal disorders—calls for immediate action. Don't say to yourself, "It'll go away." If you can't cope, GET OUTSIDE HELP IMMEDIATELY. Never let pride get in the way. Call up the Coast Guard, get the boat to the nearest port with a hospital as fast as possible or throw over the anchor and send out a distress message, either by radio or, lacking one, by flare or other visual distress signal.

You have no one to rely upon but yourself. Don't panic. Sit down and analyze the situation. Decide what you are really capable of. If the weather is deteriorating, make for the nearest port if you feel capable of the passage. Neither waste nor hoard time. Do for yourself what you would for a wife or child.

Some points to consider when abandoning ship:

- If, and only if, the mother ship is in imminent danger of sinking, inflate life raft *on deck* or by tossing overboard to activate CO_2 cylinders. Do not attempt inflation below or in the cockpit. Make sure raft is tethered before inflating. In very heavy weather the raft may flip. Do not attempt to right it until necessary.
- Extra water, food, etc. should be packed at hand in a duffel. Tie it to the raft if possible. Ship's papers, passport, etc. should be in a waterproof pouch, responsibility of the captain. If at all possible, get extra flares, radio emergency beacon and a compass aboard, as well as a chart of the area. All this takes preplanning.
- Hypothermia is one of the surest ways to quick death. Keep fully clothed, including hat and boots. Water within the oilskins will have something of a wetsuit effect, and the wet clothing, especially if

If you do go overboard and are wearing a flotation device, the best way to keep warm and alert is to assume a fetal position. Stay this way until you have your wits about you and can assess how best to get back on board.

wool, will have a high insulating effect. Move as little as possible, only so much as is necessary to stay afloat. Attempting to swim, no matter how strong a swimmer you are, will result in heat loss on a massive scale, unconsciousness and death.

• Leave the raft tethered to the ship. Too many people have been lost attempting to leap from ship to raft. Only when you are aboard should the tether be cut. Take what care you can not to cut the raft also.

• A dinghy can be used if the life raft is not functioning or if there is none. It should be fitted out beforehand, especially with a strong and sufficiently sized sea anchor to hold it bow to wind. However, since no dinghy (or virtually none) is designed for life-raft use, certain precautions are necessary. First, a rigid boat will need to be heavily fendered to avoid damage with the mother ship. Second, boarding will be extremely difficult and dangerous in anything approaching heavy seas. Third, some form of protection—canopies, dodger, etc.—will be necessary to avoid boarding seas and exposure. Fourth, permanent flotation is an absolute need. To board a dinghy, be sure to coordinate your stepping aboard with the rhythm of the two boats; otherwise you may step into thin air and descend rapidly to break limbs upon your sudden entry. Do not untether from the yacht until all members of the crew have boarded.

• If no life raft or dinghy exists, put on your life jacket, and enter the water from the windward side of the boat. From any other point the boat can drift down, or back down or slip to windward, endangering anyone in the water. Keep all clothes on, and assume a fetal position to conserve body heat. A light, whistle and knife should be attached to the life vest. Try to stay calm.

• Pickup by ship or helicopter is a dangerous, touchy and frightening maneuver. Inevitably the ship will be larger than your vessel, and the chances of collision and dismasting are great, even in calm seas. You will be distraught and tired. Try to be hoisted aboard, rather than climbing a ladder. Leave the yacht from bow or stern and time the move up to coincide with the crest of a wave. In heavy weather you will probably be safer in the lee of the larger ship, but you must move fast. Do NOT worry about your yacht! It can be replaced. Helicopter rescues demand even more thought on your part. Clear the cockpit and release any rigging located there, even if the mast goes over forward. Do NOT, repeat DO NOT, fasten the helicopter line to any part of your vessel! Grab the harness lowered, and as quickly as possible get into it. At each pass of the copter, be prepared to snag that line. In heavy seas it will be difficult, in strong winds even more so. Signal green if prepared to leave, red if not. Another possibility and perhaps safer is to be picked up from the dinghy or life raft towed astern. However, this makes you a smaller target, and gives a less stable platform for the pickup.

Some things to consider when aground:
• Backing sails can lead to accidental jibe. Be prepared. You may be better off dropping the jib and backing main. This will keep the foredeck clear for anchor handling.

● Onshore winds can vary in strength, of course. In a gale the engine will probably not be sufficiently powerful to pull you off the ground. You will have to set a kedge. Do it carefully in heavy conditions. If you plan to kedge and power at the same time be wary of fouling the propeller with the kedge warp. Either keep it taut or use floating line.

● If the tide is falling rapidly, best prepare to dry out as comfortably as possible. With fast ebb and heavy seas you may have to prepare to abandon ship, especially if the boat is on rocks.

If you get caught with the tide going out fast, try to rig a leg or two (depending on the displacement of the yacht) from oars, spinnaker poles and/or scrap lumber, lashed together and then lashed to the yacht. As the tide rolls in, you can remove it after the ship is afloat.

● If the tide is rising and you are on a lee shore, get the kedge out as fast as possible or you may be swept further ashore.

● Much depends on the profile and configuration of the boat's keel. If a long, sloping keel, you will have less trouble backing off. If a fin keel, you may be able to spin the boat about and reach or run off into deeper water. Twin-keel boats should not be heeled, as you will only increase the draft. In calm conditions, prepare to sit out the tide. In heavy going, you will have to kedge or power off.

● Heeling a single-keeled boat can be accomplished in several ways: move to the shallow water deck; swing a loaded dinghy off the boom end. In a very small boat, you may be able to use the main halyard taken ashore for leverage. (Beware: masthead fittings cannot take much abuse. Do not try this maneuver in a heavy-displacement vessel.)

• You may be able to reduce draft by lightening ship. Remove heavy gear to the dinghy, possibly drain water tanks. In a light displacement boat, this could decrease draft by the little bit needed to free the keel.

If you find yourself grounded on a shelving patch, you may be able to haul off by rowing out a kedge into deeper water, then winching the yacht off the ground. Always sound the surrounding water first—otherwise, you may find you have dragged your vessel firmer onto the hard!

• Hauling off can be done with bow anchor while transfered weight heels boat. May also be accomplished by aiding vessel. If another ship can help, first make sure that questions of salvage are resolved. Then, depending on your position, pass *your* line to the assisting vessel. Make the line secure first to foredeck bollard or stern cleats with a bridle, or secure around mast or cabin house. Instruct the other vessel to pull you slowly seaward without any surge of acceleration. This is most important. A quick application of throttle could result in torn decks or dismasting. When free and able to maneuver, request your line freed. For such tows, polypropylene cordage, since it floats, is

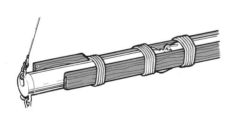

Splints for repairing a broken boom can be fashioned from fiddle rails, floorboards, an oar or spare sail battens. If your mainsail foot slides into a grooved boom, it may be reset flying, with only the clew attached to the outhaul fitting.

best employed, lessening the chances of fouled propellers.

If the boom breaks:
● Use flat-sided splints—floorboards, fiddles, bunk boards—lashed to either side of boom extending a couple of feet beyond break either side.
● If the boom is shattered or fractured beyond repair, remove it and lash a spinnaker pole, boat hook or such to the gooseneck, with the mainsail reefed. Tie reef points around jury boom.
● If gooseneck ruptures, lash inboard end of boom to mast using reefing hooks or any projection. Apply chafe protection.
● If all else fails, and you must sail without a boom, reinforce the clew and lead separate sheets to the quarters, then forward to winches by way of the spinnaker turning blocks; or, in desperation, bend sheets to the clew fitting, lash around the clew corner and lead as above.
● If foot of mainsail leads into a groove in the boom, lashing will be next to impossible, using splints. Try a boomless approach.
● If using a substitute boom, be sure to reef the mainsail. The stress on the clew will be great and you stand a good chance of ripping the clew fitting out if you do not spread the strains along the foot by tying off reef points.
● Lashing a boom to the mast without benefit of the gooseneck is a dangerous and never-easy job. Drop the main immediately, tie down boom to prevent damage to boat. Use several heavy lashings tied off independently of one another. Apply as much chafe protection as

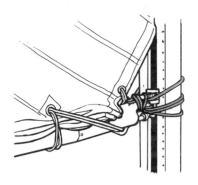

The spinnaker pole or jockey pole may be used if the boom is beyond repair. Lash the end securely with ⅜-inch (8mm) line.

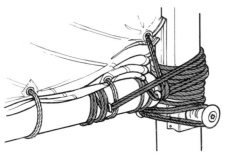

If the gooseneck breaks or explodes (it can happen), use reefing hooks or a cringle attachment shackle to lash the boom to the mast.

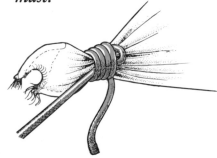

If no jury boom can be rigged, lash the clew of the mainsail securely and lead sheets to each quarter, much as you would rig a storm trysail.

107

possible, especially to the inboard end of the boom.

● Boomless jury-rigged mains are no laughing matter. You may destroy the sail without proper reinforcement. Sail shape will be distorted, and the forces on the

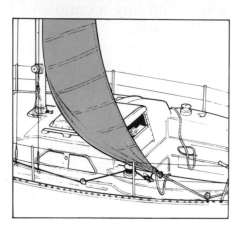

For added purchase and better leads, a boomless main may be led aft through snatch blocks shackled to the rail.

clew will be extreme. Leads can be either to turning blocks or snatch blocks on the rail. Remember that the forces are doubled and the snatch blocks and their deck attachment points must be massively robust.

● Storm trysails are remarkably efficient, rarely used sails. You should, of course, know how to set one, and have it in readiness and good repair with its sheets attached. Since it is designed to be used boomless, you have, in your sail locker, the perfect solution to a broken boom.

Some points to consider when a collision threatens:

● If bearings remain constant, chances are you are on a collision course. Taking bearings at night can be especially difficult. Try to keep one set of the approaching ship's range lights in line.

● Chances are that a large ship will not spot you until after you have spotted her.

You will probably have to take evasive action, but you should attempt to signal first:

5 or more blasts of a horn will be taken as a warning.

At night, either 5 short flashes of a strong light, or the Morse code "U" (2 short and 1 long flashes).

Also, a torch shown against the sails or a white flare will indicate your presence.

Warning signals:

One blast: I am altering course to starboard.

Two blasts: I am altering course to port.

Two blasts: *I* am going astern.

One blast: Watch out! *or* I do not comprehend your intentions.

● Evasive action does not mean sailing until you see the whites of their eyes! Make all maneuvers decisively and positively. Course changes should be large and the new course should be held. Do

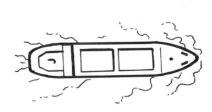

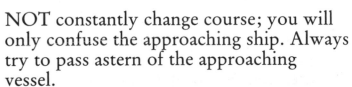

NOT constantly change course; you will only confuse the approaching ship. Always try to pass astern of the approaching vessel.

● Despite all the rules of the road, you should not hold to etiquette. Forget everything you ever learned about sail over power, etc. You should be the one to avoid the other vessel. Especially with large ships at sea, not always, but often, the watch will be shorthanded or they will

When a ship approaches, alter course to keep as clear as possible. Do not change course again until you are well clear of the ship, or until you can take bearings of the ship and note any variations in her course.

not be manning the radar, in particular with flag-of-convenience registry. Right of way is only of import if the other vessel responds in kind; otherwise, assume she is going to make mincemeat of you and act accordingly. If there is a chance of a head-on collision, both vessels SHOULD alter their courses to starboard. If the other does not, take immediate evasive action, under the fastest means possible, full throttle ahead.

● If a collision is unavoidable, try to present the smallest area of your ship as is possible to the oncoming vessel. This will,

If collision is unavoidable, you may get by with only damaged rigging if you can present the smallest possible area to the oncoming vessel. She will be going much faster than you are capable of, so be prepared for the shock of impact. Also be prepared to signal and possibly abandon ship.

it is hoped, lessen the impact and the resultant damage. If you are struck, the other vessel—if a large tanker, say—may not even know she has hit you. Get off distress flares as fast as possible. Sound horns, bells, sirens—anything to attract attention. Stand by to abandon ship. Be prepared.

Some points to consider if your vessel is dismasted:

● A mast that has gone overboard presents a serious threat to the continuing integrity of the hull, especially in heavy weather. In calm seas, you may be able to hoist the mast back on board. If the mast is sizeable and therefore heavy, a better procedure will be to lash it to the hull. Hoisting will necessitate securing the spar at at least three points along its length, and rigging tackles fore, aft and amidships—using winches in the cockpit, perhaps the vang to the maststep and the anchor windlass with appropriate jury-rigged fairleads. Be sure that the hull is appropriately fendered; in this instance, every fender aboard should be secured to the rail on the hoisting side. Chances are that the lifelines and stanchions went by the board when the mast went over, so safety harnesses are *de rigeur*. Since most masts will add considerable weight to the side to which they have been lashed, it may be necessary, especially in a light-displacement boat, to rearrange the stores and weights below deck. In addition, metal masts, unless foam-filled, will sink fairly quickly. It is imperative to move with dispatch.

● If you decide to lash the mast to the side of the yacht, a large part of the rigging will have to be cut away. This can be done

Lashing a mast alongside alone is a very difficult procedure. If the mast is reasonably buoyant, the fore end can be lashed first, then the after part. Keep spreaders vertical to avoid holing the yacht.

either by undoing the rigging screws (which will most likely be bent out of shape by the shock) or by cutting the rigging wires, either with cable cutters or with a cold chisel and hammer against a steel block. Be warned: rod rigging will not be so easy to part. That rigging which can be left—lower shrouds on the side of the vessel on which the mast went over—should be, as added security. Remember, however, that it may be necessary, in increasing heavy weather, to cut the mast adrift. Those remaining attachment points will hamper any efforts to do so.

• An additional thought: the mast can be left trailing from bow or stern to act as a sea anchor. In truly atrocious seas, this may well be the best way to retain some steerage and control. This must be accompanied by constant watch, for the errant spar could well be flung onto the ship by breaking seas. In such a case, the mast should be secured with rope cordage, rather than by rigging wire, since cutting it loose if necessary will be much simplified if an axe can take precedence over a pair of cutters.

• Should the mast fall aft, chances are anyone in the cockpit will be injured, the wheel or tiller will be broken, the cabin house may fracture. Get below and commence appropriate first aid. The mast should probably be cut away as soon as possible.

• Breaks at the spreaders are more common than one would wish to imagine. The number of fittings, terminals, etc., at that point can weaken the mast. If the mast should fracture and the upper portion come tumbling down, lash it to deck. If the mast is left dangling, lash the upper part to the portion left standing; trying to cut down the top and maneuver it to the deck can be a tricky and dangerous job.

Some points to consider about electrics:
● It is a sorry fact of life afloat that sooner or later salt air and moisture will have a detrimental effect on your boat's electrical system. You can guard against run-of-the-mill failure by checking all connections, wiring, fuses, junction boxes, circuit breakers, battery installations, etc., at the commencement of every season and at least twice during the course of the season. Battery terminals must be cleaned and, after reconnecting, coated with a thin layer of grease (waterproof). Check all wire clips to see that no breaks have occurred in the insulation. Any wires running low in the ship, especially in the bilges, should be rerouted away from any possible water contamination. Overhaul the alternator and generator. Replace all fuses and lamp bulbs as a matter of course. See that all connections and connecting clips are free from corrosion and coated after cleaning and reassembly. Top up batteries and secure. Make sure they are properly vented. Check engine wiring harnesses and make sure all wires are securely clipped and away from any excessive heat sources.
● Assuming you have done all the above and the power fails, what do you do? First check the battery. It may be dry. A connection may have vibrated or torn loose. The alternator may not be functioning. A fuse may be blown, or a cable may have shorted out.
● Having checked the above, and found the situation beyond repair, the following

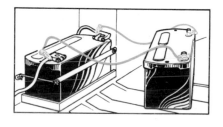

Lack of proper battery maintenance is one of the major causes of electrical failure. Terminals must be kept clean and coated to prevent the ingress of moisture. Also, batteries must be kept in a leak-proof box, well-ventilated and securely clamped down. A second battery can be wired for engine starting if necessary but a better idea would be to install a sparkproof battery switch.

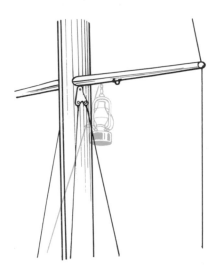

When all electrics fail, it is a good idea to keep a windproof kerosene/ paraffin lantern aboard to use as a running light or anchor light.

are all reasonable alternatives:

Use a kerosene/paraffin lantern hung in the rigging instead of navigation lights. At worst you will be thought a fisherman! Or use an electric/battery anchor light.

If the engine has no hand-crank starting capability, and a second battery is available, jump or reconnect the cables.

Sail!

Some points to consider if your gasoline engine fails:

● Check the electrical system. The battery may be dead, especially if the starter motor will not turn over. A connection between the battery ignition switch and starter motor circuit may be defective. Check the spark plugs and distributor head. Often, only the plugs will have to be replaced; always carry spares.

Basic knowledge of how a gasoline/petrol engine works is a must if your auxiliary is so equipped. The things to watch out for are dampness and poor contacts in the electrical connections.

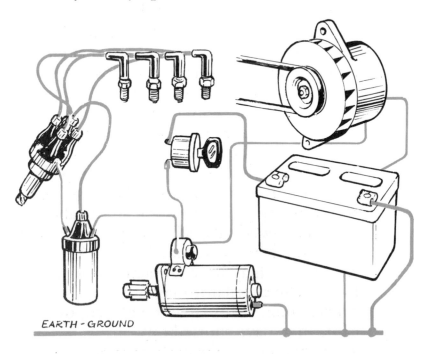

EARTH - GROUND

• If the engine stops with grinding and clanking noises, serious damage is probably at hand. If no noise occurs, an electrical fault is probable and should be traced as above. If it hesitates and stops, the fault is most likely with the fuel system. Check as per instruction manual.

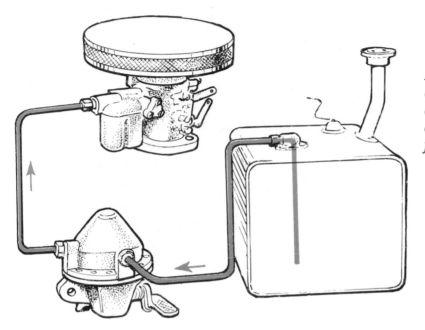

Fuel delivery systems are critical. The tank must be corrosion-free, the carburetor clean and the fuel pump running.

The fuel tank may be empty. If not, there is probably a blockage in the line, or the fuel pump may have malfunctioned. Blow out the fuel line. If still no result, dismantle or replace the pump.
• Overheating will be caused by a blocked water inlet, a broken pump, low oil level or a fouled propeller. In any case, if the temperature rises, turn off the engine immediately.
• Drop in oil pressure. Stop engine and check oil level. Refill as necessary. Do not run engine unless absolutely necessary.
• Uneven running is probably due to a fouled plug or bad timing. Replace plug. If unevenness persists, have mechanic check out.

Some points to consider if your diesel engine fails:

● If the engine stops of its own accord, switch off the ignition. Check the fuel system. Filters must be free of dirt and water. They should be filled with oil. The possibility exists that the tanks are empty. The filters may be only partly filled if this is the case. However, partial filter filling may also be due to a fuel line blockage. If the engine won't restart, you will have to bleed both filters and possibly injectors. Consult your owner's manual.

● Overheating is the most common problem with diesels and is most often due to a torn or failed water-cooling pump impeller. First, though, check the water inlet for debris and blockage. Also check the belt to the water pump. Make sure the propeller is not fouled. This is the place to

Fuel delivery is more critical in diesel engines than gasoline petrol engines. Two filters should be installed and kept clean, especially with the quality of diesel being delivered today. The tank must be checked for water infiltration and bacterial growth and the injectors must be clean and properly gapped.

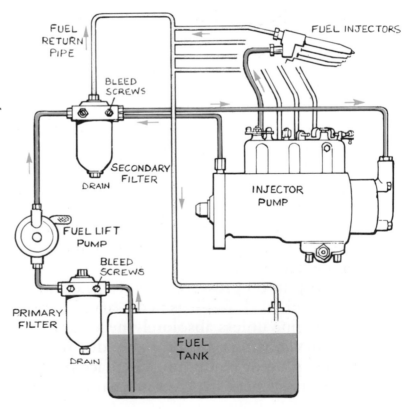

warn you: ALWAYS CARRY A SPARE IMPELLER. Changing it is a 10-minute job at most, but for want of a spare, you may be disabled until you can signal for a tow or the breeze picks up.

• Oil pressure dropping can indicate a major problem. Check the oil level and top up. If water has mixed with the oil, the head gasket may have ruptured. Do not run the engine above very low rpms (no higher than 1500 rpm in most modern marine diesels).

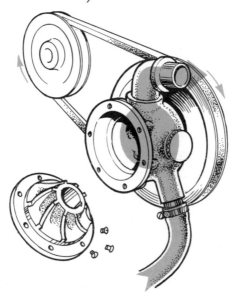

Engines can overheat and the main cause is a defective or stripped water pump impeller. Always carry a spare.

• If the engine will not start, yet the starter motor is turning over, the glow plug may need replacement.

• Uneven running may be due to a clogged or broken injector. If possible, replace; if not, run engine very slowly.

• A full spares kit as well as the manufacturer's manual should be aboard for anything more than a day sail. Read the manual before setting out on a cruise. Make sure you have the necessary tools on board. As mentioned above, should anything SEEM wrong—high temperature, rough running, frequent stoppages, oil pressure fluctuations—STOP THE ENGINE IMMEDIATELY! Failure to do so may cause major damage. Remember that anything that moves needs maintenance. As much as you might hate the "iron jib," it is part of the yacht and needs the same care as the brightwork and winches.

Some points to consider about holing:
• If you strike an object, immediately go below and check for damage. If a hole has been rent in the hull near the waterline, sail on the tack to keep the hole above water. More than likely, the hole will be hidden behind bunks or lockers or beneath immovable floorboards. There is only one solution: TEAR THE FURNITURE OUT! It hurts, but failure to do so immediately will result in probable foundering. Using a pry bar or axe or large spanner, wrench the offending woodwork (or glasswork) away.

• Use either an umbrella patch or cushions stuffed into or against the hole to stop the major flow. Another interesting possibility is to use a plumber's helper over the hole, preferably from the outside. If the hole is well below the waterline, the inflow of water will be close to twice as fast as higher up, and may be much harder to reach. The storm jib, with lines at each corner, can be passed around the hull from the outside to form a patch. Reduce the speed of the vessel to allow the sail to stay in position. Weight one corner to allow it to sink below the water with chain or odd fitments shackled together.

• No matter how hard and fast you work, a lot of water will enter the ship. The average bilge pump—25 gallons (95 litres)

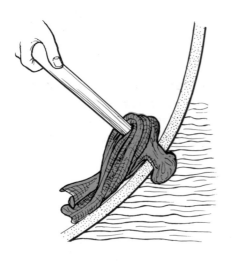

For a small hole or breach in the hull, a rag stuffed into the opening with a stick, or foam cushions pressed against the hole, may slow the influx until you are able to make permanent repairs.

per minute—will be next to useless when up against a flow of over 200 gallons (740 litres) per minute, which is what you can expect from a hole about 4 inches (10 cm) in diameter. Only a high-capacity engine-driven pump can handle a flow like that, and then only if the engine has not been flooded. But the key is speed in finding the hole and speed and efficiency in stemming the flow.

● Once the flow is stopped, or slowed to a leak, more permanent repairs can be effected. Perhaps the best material, in anything but a wooden boat, is underwater-hardening epoxy paste. Follow directions, but do try to apply on the outside first with some sort of temporary board or backing held in place. Then apply to the interior. Remember to spread the paste well past the area of the hole to allow for good surface adhesion. In a wooden ship, boards and caulking can be used to first seal the opening from within, with further repairs made from the outside when weather and conditions allow.

Some points to consider about engine fires:

● Shut off ignition immediately! Close fuel valve immediately!

● If engine room is equipped with self-

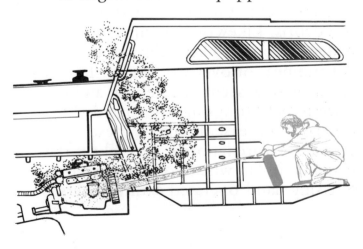

If the engine should catch fire and the ship is not fitted with an automatic extinguished system, brace yourself and use a hand-held fire extinguisher from forward of the companionway. Do NOT attempt to put it out from the cockpit as the flames will probably leap upward; you may suffer serious burns.

activating extinguishing system, stand by with an appropriate hand-operated unit. Valves have been known to corrode at sea.

• If engine room is equipped with halon extinguishing unit, close exhaust valve as soon as possible (even before shutting off ignition), as halon can be sucked out through the engine before it can work effectively.

• If no automatic unit is installed, shut off ignition *and* fuel valve, open companionway steps or engine housing, standing well clear in case of burst of flame. Direct extinguisher toward fire and release, holding it as steady as possible.

• It is vital to stop both fuel supply and ignition as soon as possible. This is especially true of gasoline/petrol engines, as explosion can occur both within the engine and back to the fuel tanks which, since they are usually located beneath or alongside the cockpit, can cause serious injury or death.

• Please, please inspect and, if necessary, replace all engine room extinguisher valves at least twice each season. Since engine spaces are usually the most ignored places aboard—at least on sailing vessels—they are subject to all the ills of bad boat husbandry: oil accumulation, severe damp, grit and old rags. Valves can not only be corroded, they can be blocked by grease and debris. Likewise, all wiring for all systems should be kept clear of the bilges, not run near or over working or hot parts of the engine, secured carefully and have all terminal fittings lightly coated with waterproof grease. If any of these precautions are ignored, very likely the system will fail when you most need it.

• Using hand-operated extinguishers is

not difficult, but does demand calm and intelligence. The important thing is to hold them steady, pointed directly at the source of the flame. If necessary, brace yourself against a bulkhead or counter.

● Engines are, of course, rarely out in the open. They are covered by hatches, companion steps or casings. If you are in the cockpit when the fire commences, get below before you open the engine compartment. You will not be able to direct your firefighting from above and, unless there is a readily removable engine hatch in the cockpit sole, don't try! Actually, cockpit engine hatches probably should not be opened, as the flames shooting out will be sure to burn you.

● If the fire gets out of control while you are below, DO NOT ATTEMPT TO ESCAPE THROUGH THE

In case of fire in the engine room, get on deck by the forward hatch. Any attempt to leave the cabin by the companionway hatch could cause serious injury.

COMPANIONWAY! Use the forward hatch, and prepare to abandon ship.

● In the event of *any* fire, prepare the life raft or dinghy to stand by. Unless you are aboard a steel or aluminum boat, the chances of a runaway blaze not causing the boat to founder are minimal. Fiberglass, unless laid-up with fire-retardant resins, will soon turn into an inferno. If you cannot contain the fire, don't fight in vain. GET OFF THE BOAT!

Some points to consider about stove fires:

● Both stove and tank valves must be closed. If stove valve cannot be reached because of flames, shut off tank valve and attempt to rip out hose. Some modern installations have remote control valves, either mechanical or electrical. These can be wired so as to simultaneously cut the fuel supply at both valve locations.

● Alcohol, though rarely used except in

An alcohol/meths stove fire may be extinguished with water. However, remember that the alcohol can be splashed about and could cause trim or fabrics to catch.

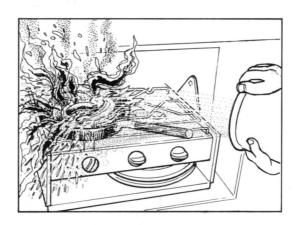

the USA, has a low flash point and *can* be extinguished with water. However, the splashing water can also carry flaming alcohol with it, possibly igniting curtains, upholstery or even the container of spirits used for preheating the burners.

● Fiberglass or other flame-retardant—treated blankets can often successfully be used to smother flames. They must be close at hand.

● Wood and coal fires can, of course, be put out with water. However, it may be handier to keep a container or bag of sand nearby. It will be safer—no steam—and

usually easier to clean up afterward: This applies to both heating and cooking stoves.
• Propane and other gas fires are the most dangerous. Flames can travel fuel lines much faster than with other fuels. A fail-safe device must be fitted to the stove, and every precaution must be made to keep all equipment in prime operating condition. Explosion is the greatest risk. If a flare-up occurs, immediately shut off the gas and apply a fire extinguisher. Use the utmost care in lighting a gas stove. Constantly check the system for gas leaks. With the exception of compressed natural gas (CNG), the entire class of fuels is heavier than air and can be ignited by the simple act of striking a wrench against the engine block.
• Keep the stove clean! A grease fire can cause just as much damage as any other. Either smother or use a fire extinguisher.

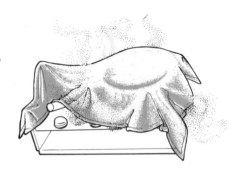

Fiberglass cloth or other flame-retardant materials can be used to smother a stove fire.

Some points to consider when caught in fog:
• Fog is usually accompanied by little or no wind. However, there are times and places where dense fog will coexist with strong breezes. In such situations, decrease throttle if under power or reduce sail more than you would normally. In dense fogs, visibility may be down to less than 300 feet (90 meters), and anything other than dead slow ahead poses a real threat to the vessel and crew.
• Human senses become less than reliable in foggy conditions: sounds are distorted, shapes appear and disappear, ships creep in and out of banks that suddenly close in. The only reliable navigational tool in such situations is the traditional ship's compass. Of course, you have made sure it is

corrected and compensated before setting out. TRUST IT! No matter what your senses indicate, the compass is a safer bet. It is not subject to psychological pressures, it doesn't drink, and it won't fall overboard.

● Fog signals: international rules:

One blast: I am turning to starboard.

Two blasts: I am turning to port.

Three blasts: I am going astern.

Five blasts: Beware!
                    I am in doubt concerning
                    your intentions.

   Short, long, short blasts: Warning! Danger of collision.

These are to be sounded on a horn or whistle. The ringing of a bell signifies a vessel aground or at anchor.

● If attempting to home in on an audible signal, remember that fog can distort apparent sound direction. Proceed with utmost caution.

● Contour navigation—following a

If caught in a fog, one possibility for safe navigation is to follow chart contours. Never trust your senses in fog. Your compass and depthsounder are your most trustworthy companions.

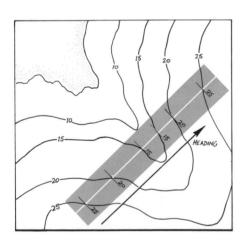

sounding line on the chart—can be most useful in fog conditions. You *must* know your position, and must have an accurate, calibrated depth finder aboard, as well as an adjusted compass with deviation table.

You then proceed to take soundings in a continuous run in the charted direction. Any deviation from the charted sounding line will become immediately apparent from the soundings.

- Radar is not often found aboard small yachts, but recent developments are putting it in the range of affordability, and scanner size and power requirements are decreasing. Radar takes practice, but if you have a set, you will no doubt have figured out how to use it. Depending on range, it can show you exactly what is ahead of you in most, if not all, conditions.

Some points to consider about lee shores:

- Under most conditions a lee shore should be avoided only because of the possibility of heavy weather. If no choice exists, try to anchor as far out as is possible with safety.
- If the engine is powerful, motor sailing should be attempted before trying to leave under sail alone.
- In truly horrendous conditions, boats have survived by sailing in a half-circle and dropping as many anchors as are on board. Under these conditions it will not be possible to set anything from the dinghy and no other choice will exist.
- Careful planning and coordination will be necessary for these maneuvers to work. It will be difficult to keep the headsail from flogging itself to death and the jib sheets from fouling. However, your safety depends on this. Try to lower the jib as soon as the anchor line has been released.
- When alone or shorthanded, it may be an advantage to sail the yacht out under only one sail—whichever is most

efficient—keeping the decks relatively clear. If you must lose an anchor, do so it costs less than the ship.

Some points to consider about life rafts:
- It should be obvious that a life raft must be kept on deck or in a special raft locker. Nevertheless, many yachtsmen place it in a cockpit or lazaret locker where accumulations of gear and debris block access to it. Under-the-sole lockers are not recommended for easy access. Best location is either lashed to the coachroof fore or aft of the mast, or on the afterdeck or beneath the helmsman seat. Some newer boats have special recesses within the transom; these are fine if, in practice, you can get to them without endangering yourself. Best to keep all safety gear inboard if possible.
- Don't use lashings that end up like the Gordian knot. They must be slashable with one stroke of a knife, or with a single tug on a line—some variant of a slippery hitch, for example. The lashings are best done up in natural cordage, as synthetics will slip too much. Manila or hemp—if you can find it—are good. Patent hold-down systems can be acceptable, providing they are constantly checked for corrosion or chafe. Like anything mechanical, they are liable to seizure and breakdown when most needed.
- Servicing is vital to life raft performance. Kept on deck, the raft, even in a fiberglass cannister, is subject to moisture penetration, fabric deterioration and valve failure. Yearly servicing by an authorized service center is vital. Yes, it is expensive. Yes, you need to do it. While we are on the subject, do buy a cannister raft. Valises are too subject to kicks,

seepage and puncture. They should be avoided at all costs, no matter how well-protected you believe the raft to be. Also, pay more and get a raft that is up to SOLAS standards. The difference, especially offshore, is worth it both in terms of construction and materials specifications and in terms of equipment.

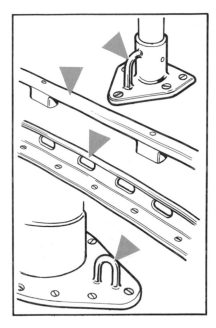

● Depending where the raft is located, the painter should be tied to a deck fitting which is *through-bolted*. The strains upon raft and painter in rough seas when the raft is thrown overboard are great. Stanchion bases, mast step, coachroof rails, pushpit are all appropriate choices.

● NEVER ATTEMPT TO INFLATE THE RAFT WHILE IT IS ON BOARD! What with rigging, deck gear, wheel or tiller, etc., you will never be able to get it into the water, and if you do, the chances are you will rip the fabric or tear off a fitting or two. Always throw it clear of the ship.

Attachment points for life rafts must be through-bolted and strong. They will ultimately have to hold the raft against great strains, both when it is on deck and when it is tossed overboard.

● The painter can become tangled. First make sure it is clear, then tug firmly. The throw of the raft may start inflation, but it is always best to make sure by giving the painter the approved and appropriate pull. If the raft does not inflate, or only partially fills, start pumping. Make sure that you are secure in a safety harness.

● Should abandonment of the mother vessel become imperative, board the raft before cutting the painter. Rafts drift—especially in the conditions likely prevail at the time—at a remarkable rate. There is little or no chance that contact can be reestablished with the yacht.

Some points to consider about lightning:
● Lightning is always unpredictable. Though it will rarely strike a yacht,

enough cases exist, especially along the American eastern seaboard, to take all possible precautions. Since it will follow the most direct path to the water, it is up to you to provide such a path to help it on its way.

● Though #8 copper wire is generally recommended for a lightning ground, much better is to use copper tubing,

Lightning protection should be arranged so that all shrouds, mast, stays and rails are tied to a common ground.

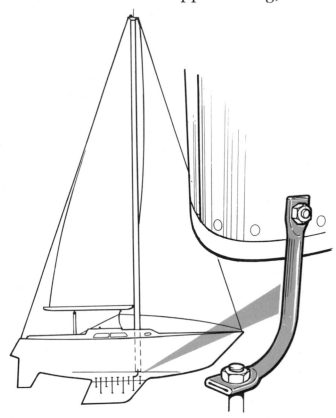

flattened at the ends, connecting the lightning rod at the masthead with a keel bolt. In a boat with an encapsulated keel, a grounding plate should be attached to the hull as low below the waterline as is feasible.

● Since very few European boats are fitted with lightning protection, in a sudden storm a length of chain, shackled to the cap shroud and dangled overboard (make sure it is long enough to remain under water) will act as a satisfactory substitute. If time exists, tape the shackle end of the chain to the shroud to ensure positive contact.

● Obviously, the helmsman remains in great danger especially if steering with a wheel. If possible, anchor; when at sea, heave to and get below.

Some points to consider about lights:

● If the lights aboard go, hoist a lantern, preferably on the backstay. If hoisted to the spreaders, it will not be seen from leeward.

● Despite the International Rules, incorrect lights are often shown. Fishing boats are prime culprits, but yachts and merchant ships can also be offenders.

● Always attempt to discern exactly what lights are being shown where on an approaching vessel before taking evasive action. Likewise, even in approved anchorages, always hoist an anchor light.

● Strobe lights, NOT in accordance with the International Rules, should be used only for distress and then only when necessary, as they can confuse a watch officer on the bridge of a large ship.

Some points to consider about bilge pumps:

● Most modern bilge pumps are of the diaphragm type. These will function in situations where older pumps would have long failed or clogged. However, even a pump which has a capacity of moving 30 gallons per minute (115 l) will not be very effective with a major hull breach. In such a case, only an engine-driven pump will suffice. And if the engine ceases to function, a bucket brigade will do far more than either.

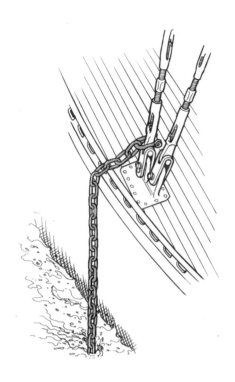

In lightning emergencies, a length of chain shackled to a chainplate or rigging screw can substitute for proper internal grounding. Be sure the chain is long enough to stay in the water no matter how violently the ship may roll.

Proper pump mounting means it can be used either at the helm or from below. Ideally, two pumps will be fitted.

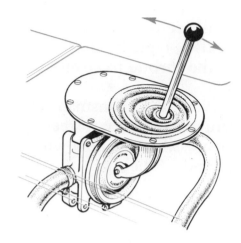

• Always carry spares for all pumps. A new diaphragm can be installed in approximately five minutes, providing access is reasonable. The same is true of strainers; you must be able to reach them.

• Installation is vital to proper pump efficiency and safety. Too often, bilge pumps are mounted so that a cockpit locker lid must be opened to operate them. Mount cockpit pump with a through-deck fitting, properly capped and watertight and accessible to the helmsman. Any offshore boat should have a second pump operable from below. Most stock boats are equipped with pumps of much too small capacity. Minimum should be 25 gallons per minute (95 l).

• Pump handles will break. Either keep a factory spare or make sure the interior and exterior pumps have identical handles and carry a hardwood dowel of correct dimensions. Also, it is a good idea to drill a hole through the handle and tie it with a light lanyard to a spot where it is always at hand, near the pump. A spring clip will also work well.

Some points to consider should the rigging fail:

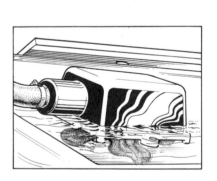

A strum box or intake filter must be fitted to prevent pumps from clogging. In turn, this should be readily accessible for cleaning and clearing.

● Depending on conditions, you can continue sailing. However, if its calm and forestay fails, best let well enough alone, rather than risk the chance of the mast's falling aft into the cockpit. When things start getting rough such luxuries will not be possible, and getting the sails down and the rigging break mended will be most important. If the backstay breaks, lead a halyard aft and tension with a Spanish windlass or block and tackle—the vang, perhaps. You will head up during this process, needless to say. If the forestay ruptures, head downwind, then use a spare halyard shackled to the stemhead for support. If long enough, this can be led aft to a winch for greater tensioning and security.

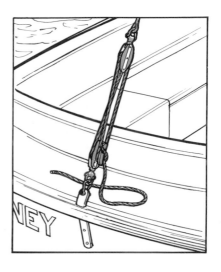

A vang or tackle arrangement can be used to repair a broken backstay, often in conjunction with a spare halyard led aft.

● Should a shroud go, immediately tack—jinbing will place undue strain on the rig, and could carry it away—and head off so as to put the least strain on the failed part of the rig. Try to take sea state into account, as undue pitching and rolling can cause almost as much damage as the original fitting's letting go.

● Your most useful equipment for jury rigging, besides a spare halyard, will be wire rope or bulldog clips. These should be galvanized, not stainless steel, which has a tendency to slip. If a stay has fractured at the turnbuckle fitting end, form a bight or loop with the wire and use at least two clips to form an eye, which can be lashed or shackled to the turnbuckle or attached directly to the chainplate with a block and tackle. If the stay has broken at the masthead, sooner or later you shall have to go aloft. If no spare length of wire is aboard, the eye should be made at the end of wire aloft (do this while

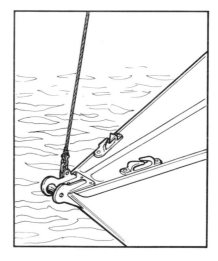

Likewise, a spare or spinnaker halyard can double as a temporary headstay.

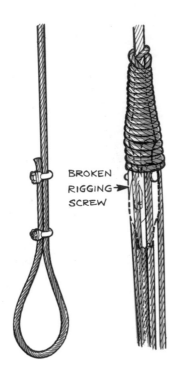

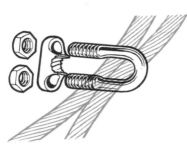

If an end fitting should go by the board, lashings can be used or wire rope clamps-bulldog clamps can be utilized to make loops with thimbles or to sieze two wires together. They should be of galvanized steel, since stainless steel has a tendency to slip against the wire.

still on deck), which can then be shackled to the masthead fitting or tang. The now shorter stay can be attached to the chainplate or turnbuckle with shackles and a length of chain. If the wire has broken midway, make two eyes and fasten them with shackles, lashings or chain.

• Rarely does it occur, but when a turnbuckle fractures or lets go, the solution is actually much simpler than when the shroud or stay breaks. Simply replace it with another turnbuckle, use a lanyard or lash the stay in place. Times come, though, when the turnbuckle is frozen tight. This is due to lax maintenance, and you should curse yourself roudly. Since you are presumably sailing on a tack that takes the strain off the fitting, remove the offender by slipping a clevis, lash the stay temporarily, and use two mole wrenches to break the freeze. Replace.

• Should wire need to be cut, use either wire cutters or a cold chisel. However, first whip or tape the wire to either side of the proposed cut to prevent unlaid strands or eye-damaging bits of flying steel. Wire rope is prone to a life of its own, and a vise should be used to hold it fast.

Some points to consider about distress signaling:

• Far too often distress signals are sent for inappropriate reasons or for no reason at all. If the engine has died and you are merely becalmed, *no* reason exists to send any signal. Patience is the solution.

• Don't use flares in the daytime and smoke signals at night. Don't use an EPIRB when 5 miles (8 km) from port. Don't attempt using VFH distress channel in midocean. Common sense should dictate the signal most appropriate for any situation.

● Equally a question of propriety, don't waste signals, especially pyrotechnics. Unless you are near land, or sight another ship, chances are your visual signal will not be seen. This is especially true of open water passages, a great many of which are away from shipping lanes.

● Pyrotechnics, either hand-held or fired, must be used with caution. If any way exists to practice legally, avail yourself of it. When the time comes to use them, do so without panic. Potentially fatal accidents can and have occurred. The chance of starting a fire exists. Always set off flares away from tanks, gas bottles, engines, etc.

● In a pinch, a metal bucket of flaming

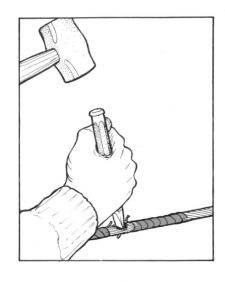

If you must cut wire, either cutters or a cold chisel will work. In either case, be sure the ends are tied to a rail or padeye. Whipping wire can cause serious injury.

Hand-held pyrotechnics must be used with care, away from sails and with foreknowledge. Many manufacturers now make practice flares, which are legal for testing your skills.

rags, a gun fired and, most important, a signal mirror can work. Obviously, the burning materials must be used with extreme caution, and are not advised aboard GRP boats. A signal mirror, even if torn from the head's bulkhead, can, providing the weather cooperates, be

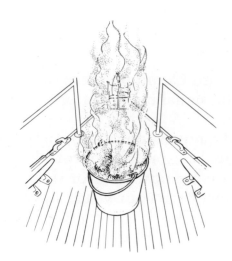

In emergencies, a bucket of oily rags set afire on the foredeck will signify you are in distress. Remember to try this only in a steel bucket with some sort of fireproof protection under the bucket—and never leave the bucket unattended. This procedure is only appropriate in calm conditions.

A signalling mirror is still one of the best ways to attract attention, especially to the bridge of a passing ship.

extremely effective. It is seen from the bridge of a large ship with greater ease than dye markers or other daytime visual signals.

● IMPORTANT: all signals must be used with caution, calm and a regard for the realities of the seas. If you can—whatever the manner—get safely to port, do so on your own. The cost to others should be considered before haphazardly requesting assistance.

Some points to consider should the tiller break:

● Outboard rudder: jam a section of boathook or an oar between the rudder cheeks and lash in place.
● Outboard rudder: if tiller fits to either side of rudder blade, lash poles or scrap wood around blade top.
● Inboard rudder: cheek-type fitting, like first suggestion above.
● Inboard rudder: socket fitting, opening may not be clearable. Use visegrip/molegrip pliers with lines led to coaming blocks and thence to winches.
● Cheeks at rudder head may also be damaged. Scrap plywood can be used as reinforcement on either side, lashed temporarily. Later, when time permits, drill three staggered holes through ply and

rudder cheeks and bolt through. Makeshift tiller can still be lashed between the new cheeks or drilled and through-bolted, making for a stronger, more responsive jury tiller.

● If nothing else is at hand, use two long fiddles, such as are often found keeping settee cushions in place. These are usually fastened with self-tapping screws and can easily be refitted later; they make an

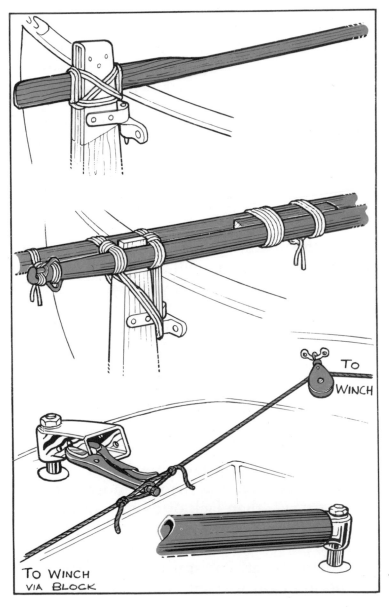

TO
WINCH

TO WINCH
VIA BLOCK

Any number of jury rigs can be devised for a broken tiller. Here are three easily rigged possibilities.

elegant, either-side-of-the-rudder-head tiller.

- Cheek fittings are usually bronze or stainless steel and the wood may have swelled between them, the tiller having broken slightly above the fitting. Knock out retaining bolt and swollen wood fragments. This will require a chisel and mallet. The same tools can be used to shape the wood replacement. Remember, any jury tiller will be weaker and offer a less than ideal position for maximum leverage. Go easy.
- Socket fittings are usually impossible to clear quickly. A possible solution is to use a section of whisker/jockey pole or any strong tubing *over* the socket fitting. Another possibility, if you can clear the socket, is to use a spare stanchion, chilly to touch but of unrivaled strength.

Medical Emergencies

Some information about medical emergencies (*Note*: The following will apply to both singlehanders and crewed yachts):
- Do you need to save a life?
- Do you need to prevent the situation from worsening?
- Must you relieve pain and suffering?
- Do you need outside assistance?
- If the person has stopped breathing or has no discirnable heartbeat, you must act immediately to save that person's life. Bleeding will kill a person much less quickly—unless it is a major hemorrhage of a major artery—than lack of oxygen or no heartbeat.
- If the person is not subject to any immediate threat, you must decide if the condition might worsen. Many injuries

and illnesses can get more serious, but the most common might include: burns; infections; exposure; poisoning; concussion; unconsciousness; fractures; open wounds; chest pain. If you decide that the person is in no immediate danger, continue to port. Otherwise, consult your medical guide.

• The greatest concurrent problem with any injury at sea may be fear. Not only take appropriate action but also reassure the injured person. Care, concern and will can play as important a part as anything to help alleviate distress and aid someone on the path to recovery.

• Can you cope? Certain medical conditions will be beyond your ability to treat. If you are far from shore, you must use your judgement and common sense, and do everything in your power to aid the patient with what you have at hand. Certain infections can be held at bay with antibiotics. Certain fractures can be immobilized until a doctor is at hand. But other conditions may be impossible to do much about. Internal hemorrhaging, heart attack, certain types of poisoning, extreme hypothermia may be beyond anything you can do. You can but try.

Following are some general guidelines for treatment and diagnosis. They should be used in conjunction with a reliable medical first-aid manual. They are not infallible, and any responsibility is in the hands of the person administering the first aid.

Abdominal pain. This can be mild or severe. Until the cause is clear:
   Put the patient to rest.
   Allow neither food nor liquids.

Do not give laxatives.

Give pain medication if required. If pain is persistent, vomiting frequent, diarrhea severe, abdomen firm and tender, seek medical assistance. Very severe pain accompanied by very hard, tender abdomen can indicate ruptured appendix, ulcer or ovarian cyst. Infection is possible, and antibiotics every 6 hours should be considered until professional advice is secured.

Antibiotics do *not* cure everything! They are useless against viral or fungal infections. Follow doctor's recommendations closely as to dosage and types to carry aboard. Duration of treatment should be no more than a week to 10 days. Cautions:

Avoid sunlight.

Never give to pregnant women or children under 8 without specific medical advice.

Allergic reactions or lack of response should indicate need for immediate medical consultation.

Bleeding. The only pressure point that matters is directly over the bleeding area. Use sterile, soft, absorbent material. Small cuts will usually stop bleeding after a short while; larger cuts should have the material taped over until further action can be taken. Cleanse with soap and water or with hydrogen peroxide. Only use a tourniquet in emergencies for extremely heavy bleeding.

Burns. For all burns, the immediate treatment is to apply cold water liberally. Use soaked cloths, either fresh or salt. Avoid running water and ointments, creams or sprays. With anything more than a first-degree burn, cover with sterile petroleum jelly, gauze and a sterile dressing. For second- and third-degree burns, seek immediate

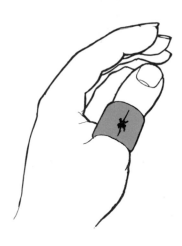

Small cuts can be firmly taped with a sterile bandage.

medical attention. Life-threatening burns can cause shock and the danger of infection. Take fluids orally, keep dressings in place, take pain killers and antibiotics if more than 24 hours will elapse before a doctor can care for you.

Cardiopulmonary arrest. Heart attack or lung malfunction. Follow these steps:

Should you have crew aboard, determine consciousness.

Open the airway, tilt back the head with neck lifted.

Give mouth-to-mouth resuscitation; if after four breaths the chest doesn't move, attempt Heimlich maneuver.

Feel for pulse; if there but no breathing start mouth-to-mouth at one breath per 5 seconds.

If no pulse, start *CPR* Your local Red Cross offers training in this lifesaving technique. If you haven't taken the course, follow the steps below only if the situation is genuinely desperate:

Place victim on hard surface.

Place the heel of the hand over the sternum about 2 inches (5 cm) from the lower tip.

Place other hand at right angles on top of the first and press down hard enough to depress the breastplate an inch or two (2 or 5 cm). Release. Pause. Repeat.

Give victims 2 breaths after each 10 to 15 depressions.

Choking. Use the Heimlich maneuver:

Deliver back thumps with a closed fist between the shoulder blades.

With hands clasped around the victim, make abdominal thrusts between the breastplate and the navel—4 thumps, 4 thrusts. Continue until choking is relieved.

Cold. Wear loose-fitting warm clothes;

keep hands, feet and head covered. Get out of wet clothes as soon as possible. Drink and eat warm substances. Do NOT drink alcohol. *Frostbite*. Warm affected part rapidly in water at 104°F (40°C). Pain medication may be needed. Seek medical assistance; if unavailable, warm soaks twice a day, clean dressings and separation of toes and fingers will prevent tissue deterioration.

Constipation. Eat lots of fruits, vegetables and roughage (fiber). Colace tablets are usually effective and convenient to take. Avoid laxatives. A glycerin suppository or a warm-water enema may be best for prolonged constipation.

Cuts. Use strip or butterfly bandages to close the cut, apply pressure and keep it clean. Larger cuts will require stitching and prompt medical attention. If signs of infection appear, use antibiotics.

Diarrhea. Keep up fluid intake; most patent medicines will make the patient feel better but will not *cure* the cause. Pepto-Bismol may be the best, according to a recent study. If the diarrhea is accompanied by high fever or bloody stools, use ampicillin as per directions. Seek medical care as soon as possible, as complications are possible.

Eyes. For eye irritations, glare, foreign bodies: wash with fresh water, cover with loose-fitting bandages. Seek medical care if pain or visual impairment persists. Always wear sunglasses.

Fever. Use aspirin or acetaminophen, no more than 10 grains every 4 hours. Do NOT increase dosage. Cool sponge baths can aid in reducing fever. Dress lightly unless suffering chills. If fever is high and persists, infection is possible and antibiotics are called for. If no change after 48 hours, seek immediate medical attention.

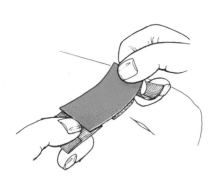

Larger cuts can be closed using wide sterile bandages or butterfly closures.

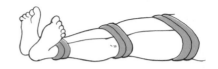

Fractures. Immobilize immediately. Apply ice packs if possible. Give pain medication. Do NOT try to set the fracture, merely keep it from moving with splints or bandages. Keep tight enough but not so tight as to stop or hinder circulation. Seek medical aid immediately. Compound fractures—where skin has been broken—will require cleansing of the wound and antibiotics.

Heat. Keep protected, even on cool days. Drink what you need to feel comfortable. Do NOT ration water. The body can store water and the old saw about rationing has been fairly convincingly disproved by recent U.S. Army Survival School studies. If heatstroke occurs, intensive, rapid cooling is called for. Put victim in cold-water bath (plugged cockpit) or wrap in soaked sheets. Seawater works well. After body temperature has dropped to 102°F (38.9°C), cease cold treatment. Massage arms and legs to promote cooling circulation. As soon as possible start taking cool liquids by mouth. Follow-up medical care is necessary, as potentially serious damage can be inflicted on internal organs.

Pain. Pain is a symptom. Specific medication will not cure the cause unless the cause is known. For relief: aspirin, acetaminophen. For medium pain, codeine, Darvon, Percodan, Talwin; these all require prescriptions. Ask your doctor for specifics. Severe and persistent pain: morphine or Demerol. These are dangerous drugs and should be avoided for all but the transoceanic passagemaker. Ask for specifics from your doctor.

Poisoning. *Internal*: cause vomiting as soon as possible, except for petroleum products; after vomiting stops, take milk, mineral oil or bread to absorb the poison and

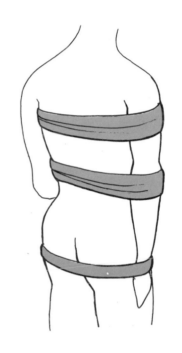

Fractures or possible fracture must be kept immobile. Bandages or splints and bandages can be used as shown.

keep it from absorption into the system. *Skin contact*: wash thoroughly with water, remove clothing. *Breathing*: get into fresh air immediately. So many poisons exist it is well to contact a doctor by radio as soon as you are able to. He or she may be able to help. If victim is comatose, get to land immediately, even if it means calling for air rescue.

Respiratory infections. The infection cures itself. Flu, colds, sore throat, bronchitis are best treated with rest, lots of fluids, aspirin, decongestants, etc. In cases where fever develops or persists and no improvement is seen, antibiotics may be called for. They should be kept up for 10 days, even after symptoms have disappeared.

Seasickness. The most effective medication I known is Bucladin. This is a prescription drug better known in the U.K. than in the U.S.
Patent medicines work or don't work according to the individual. Chronic seasickness must be dealt with as best as one can. Milder forms can often be cured by focusing on a distant horizon, keeping blood sugar levels up, and avoiding interiors or exaggerated sense of motion.

Shock. Shock can follow any severe injury, particularly serious burns or blood loss. It is an indication of internal bleeding. The victim will be pale, faint and sweaty with a weak, rapid pulse and cold, moist skin. He may be thirsty, drowsy and confused; he will eventually lose consciousness. Shock is fatal unless treated, yet there is little one can do without medical facilities. *Summon help immediately!* Lay the victim on his back and raise the legs about 1 foot (30 cm) with cushions or the like. Keep the victim warm.

Urinary infections. *Nonspecific*: drink lots of fluids; pyridium can be administered to

relieve burning and frequency of urination.
Wait a week before administering anything
else. If infection persists, administer Gantrisin
or tetracycline. Seek medical advice. *Specific*
(venereal): gonorrhea symptoms—discharge,
burning urination—are treated with
antibiotics and medical follow-up.

10. Repairs

If you sail regularly and often, you will at
some point be faced with the necessity of
making repairs at sea. It may be something as
simple as tying a bowline to replace a chafed
splice, or it may be a far more momentous
task . . . replacing a rudder or rigging a jury
mast. Then again, many sailors voyage for
50 years without ever experiencing the
slightest problem. The odds, however, are
against you. To cope, one must have
knowledge, spares and tools, and techniques.

Knowledge is a curious thing with sailors.
Most quickly become "experts," at least
around the clubhouse bar. Real knowledge
comes with experience, real experience on the
water, not that of reading books like this. A
bold thing for an author say, yet having
devoured hundreds of volumes nautical, I still
had to think through the problem of getting
off my first grounding on a sandbar. The first
thing that happens when an emergency arises
is to shout several obscenities at random,
heard only by the gods. This is usually
followed by a great amount of strenuous
movement hither and yon searching for
things which can never be found. Finally, in
panic, you call for aid and assistance.

The above scenario, though it lapses into farce, is not too far off the mark for many sailors. It is a sad commentary on our various nautical traditions. Unlike a car, which can be fixed (after a fashion) almost anywhere, a yacht at sea—or even in a secluded cove—must be the TOTAL responsibility of her skipper. This does not mean you must be a master mechanic, but if you wish to sail without a supply ship alongside, it would be a good idea to have a rudimentary working knowledge of all systems on board.

In other words, to be prepared, you must know what to be prepared for! Simply put, there are several broad catagories to familiarize yourself with:

1. Hull structure and deck bond
2. Steering apparatus
3. Powerplant
4. Sails and rigging
5. Plumbing
6. Electrics and miscellaneous luxuries.

For want of a horse, a battle was lost, and for want of a sound hull, the ship will founder. Thousands of yachts are churned out yearly by hundreds of yards. The rule never changes: you get what you pay for. A cheap daysailer is not meant to be sailed across oceans. It is not up to the task structurally or ergonomically. Assuming you have a recognizably good ship which has been properly surveyed, you, as the skipper, should not only recognize it on a mooring. You must know the location of every through-hull, each keel bolt, all stringers, how the furniture and ceilings are attached, how you might be able to get to a low and inconvenient part of the hull in case of a holing. If this seems like a daunting task, I strongly recommend that you take up croquet or some sport which demands little in the way of structural and physical knowledge. Things are going to get far more complicated.

Some points to consider to counter chafe:

- A sheetbend is the quickest way to take care of serious chafe, though it must be remembered that knots will never be as strong as the original or as a splice. Using two bowlines will have the advantage of easy undoing of the knots no matter how heavy the strain on the lines.

Bowlines make for a strong connection between two lines. They will not pass through a sheave, of course.

- The easiest thing to do is to end-for-end the line, although, depending on the application, this can cause further chafe and weakening of the line. However, with modern fiber rope this is rarely a problem, and top-quality polyester rope will last as long as 20 years with proper care. Better, get rid of the original cause of the chafing: unfair leads, rough edges (the application of a fine-toothed file will achieve wonders, especially on metal fittings), etc.
- Padding—whether by plastic tubing or by hose, rags, leather, a sacrificial rope whipping or baggywrinkle—is as old a

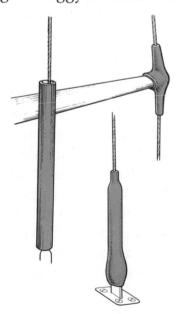

Modern, streamlined chafe protectors are certainly to be preferred to the baggywrinkle of old.

A long splice is the best way to repair any running rigging. Short splices will not pass through blocks.

practice as the sailor has. Where sail chafe is involved, the best recourse is to have the sail recut or reinforced. Baggywrinkle is ugly, soils the sails, and creates a surprising amount of windage. Better is to use shroud rollers or spreader tips. No matter what material is chosen, the padding must be secured, either with tape or whipping.

● The most secure method of repairing a chafed line, short of replacing the line altogether, is to cut and splice it. A short splice will be stronger but will not be able to pass through a block sheave; a long splice will be close to the original diameter of the line and will pass, providing the sheave is large enough in the first place.

Some points to consider about rigging a jury mast:

● Depending upon the damage inflicted to the mast, a jury rig may be an addition to what remains standing or it may be an entire make-do structure. If the mast has broken above the spreaders, the storm trysail may work as a mainsail with only a forestay and backstay pieced together from spare wire and wire rope clips. If only the mizzen remains, a forestay can be fashioned—albeit at a very low angle—and a jib can be modified to be set flying from said stay. As along as the remaining bit of mast has retained the lower shrouds, a low-efficiency sailing rig is not only possible but relatively simple to fabricate.

● If the mast breaks at or near deck level, a different set of criteria apply. First see what is salvageable from the leavings of your once noble spar. It may be possible to save stays, hardware or a section of the spar itself. Before you decide what you

If the mast is useless in the normal position on deck, an "all-headsail" rig can be improvised. If it is partially standing, the storm trysail can help keep you going.

will do, see what you have to work with.
• Having made an inventory of working materials—not forgetting oars, spinnaker and jockey poles, bunk fronts, etc.—sit below with a clean sheet of paper, some basic measurements (base of foretriangle, length of longest usable mast section, length of various salvaged wire, etc.) and a pencil and see what *might* be possible— what L. Francis Herreshoff called "thought experiments." It will be much easier than trying different combinations on deck in a seaway at night with the wind

at force 6. Perhaps the most important thing to remember is that the rig you design must be able to be created, hoisted and used by the available manpower and the available skills. If you are within sight of land, turn on the engine! However, if you are midocean, you will want to devise something that will take you where you want to go on the available rations and water aboard in whatever weather you may reasonably expect.

- Having come up with a solution, collect and assemble all the necessary parts. Do as much as possible with the new rig *on deck.* The less needed to be done aloft, the safer. Make sure, for example, that all the "masthead" fittings are secured, that the correct length wires and ropes are tied off. You don't want to have to lower the whole mess if you can avoid it.

A tripod arrangement can be devised to raise your jury rig. Be sure to think it all out before you start to improvise.

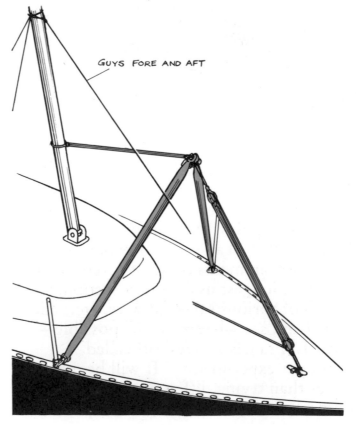

GUYS FORE AND AFT

● Depending on its size and weight, raising of the rig can be a job for one with a winch and a tripod arrangement or for the muscles of 10 strong men. Obviously, you wish to get the thing up with minimal effort.

● Setting sail may mean adopting some odd and backended configurations. Jibs

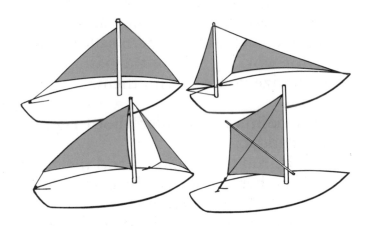

Here are several possible jury rigs. How they might work on your yacht depends on deck layout, available materials and body strength.

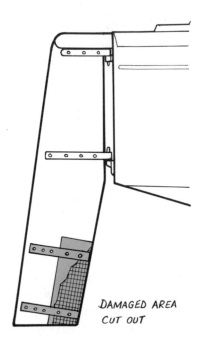

DAMAGED AREA
CUT OUT

If your rudder breaks only partially, you may be able to patch it with strapping and sheet metal or wood. Its effectiveness will depend on where the break is and how smooth you can make the leading and trailing edges. The key is to make sure that the repaired rudder will be close to the depth of the original.

may be turned on end, or sewn together. Storm sails may be the best driving sails for a reduced rig, and setting them flying may be the best, and safest, means of propulsion. What is most important is to devise a sail combination that will get you where you wish to go. Quite often sprit-sails, lateen rigs, makeshift schooners and square sails will serve the purpose quite well—if you know anything about them. Unfortunately, the modern sailor has little use for working sails of the past. Try to familiarize yourself with them.

Some points to consider about rigging a jury rudder:
• If the rudder is inboard and the stock has been bent, ignore it. Instead, you will have to fashion a rudder or sweep to work off the transom. If the blade is damaged, it may still be possible to steer the boat, albeit with reduced sail. However, if response is minimal and you are some distance from port, some sort of rudder will have to be constructed.
• Should the steering gear be damaged beyond repair, an emergency tiller should be aboard. Since many more yachts are wheel-steered now than even 20 years ago, essential spares should be carried—cable, clamps, sprocket wheels, gears, etc. Obviously, you will never be covered for all contingencies. And, sooner or later, you will have to rig that emergency tiller. Accidents do happen which will incapacitate both wheel and rudder. Jury rudder again.
• The simplest repairs are to a transom-hung rudder, which can be shipped and patched, or even replaced from parts fashioned from floorboards, hatch boards,

etc. If the pintles and gudgeons are not bent or broken, repairs should be fairly straightforward, and if the rudder is wood can be accomplished with screws and bolts. If the rudder is fiberglass, the same methods can be used but reinforcement will be necessary in the form of load-spreading washers (of metal or wood) and lashings. However, if the major portion of the blade has been torn away, and the fastenings between rudder and hull are without integrity, a new rudder assembly will have to be fashioned.

• Inboard rudders pose a different set of problems. If the rudder bearing has been broken, and the rudder is slamming back and forth, potential exists for major hull damage or rupture, especially in a seaway. Some means of locking the rudder in position will have to be devised, or even of shipping the entire assembly. One good precaution is to drill a small hole in the trailing edge of the blade, with the foreknowledge that this will be used—should an emergency occur—to lead lines outboard and to the cockpit for steering. If the blade can be set, a rudder aft will still have to be fashioned.

• Some self-steering wind vanes can be adapted to act as an auxiliary rudder. This potential might well be investigated when you contemplate the purchase of a vane.

• To actually construct a new rudder, first gather the necessary materials: a pole—boom, spinnaker pole, oar (if long enough); a blade substitute such as a hatch board or section of floorboard; line, lashings, bolts, tools needed, etc. Fasten the pole to the blade with through-bolts, U bolts, or anything which will produce a rigid structure. Next, determine how to

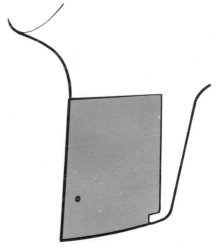

Plan ahead as much as possible. You could have a predrilled hole in the rudder blade. Should you then lose the tiller, a line can be rigged to the cockpit to allow steering by means of blocks and the lines led to the helm.

151

Singlehanding

If the rudder cannot be repaired, jury systems can be worked out using boards, oars, lashings, spinnaker poles, etc. Here are several examples. The most difficult thing will be to attach the sweep to the stern of the yacht. Some sort of lashing will probably work best, but make sure it is strong and heavy, since there will be a lot of chafing.

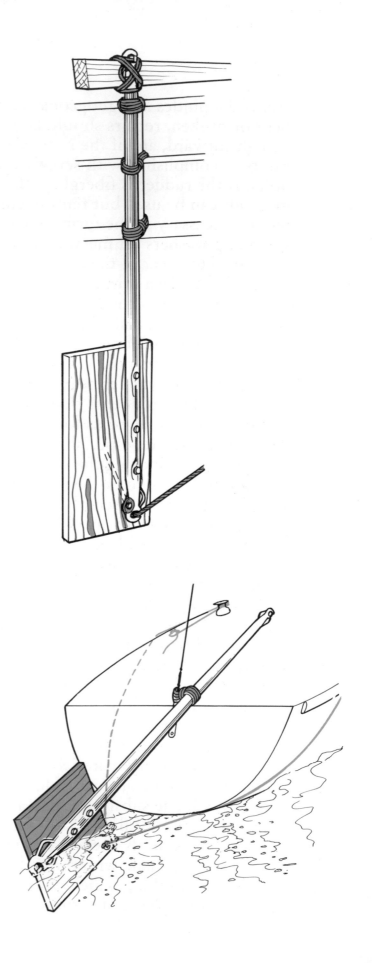

attach the assembly to the stern. As long as the blade will be deeply immersed, any method will do. However, the stern's shape will determine the most appropriate way of accomplishing this.

● Perhaps the easiest stern to mount your new rudder on will be virtually plumb, utilizing the pushpit horizontals as fastening points, with stout lashings to hold the two together. Reverse-counter transoms will demand a more deck-level approach, with some fitting being used to hold the lashing. Traditional forward-sloping counters will best use the pushpit as above. Lacking guard rails aft, deck-level lashings will have to be used, remembering that with a single-point lashing some means will have to be devised to hold the blade in the water. Ballasting is one possibility. Another is to run lines from a hole in the *forward* edge of the blade near the bottom, outboard and forward to strong points on deck. The backstay can also be used as a second lashing point for the pole/stock, remembering that any lashing used here will put enormous strains on the entire rig and should be used warily in heavy weather.

● To ease steering, lines can be led through snatch blocks attached to the

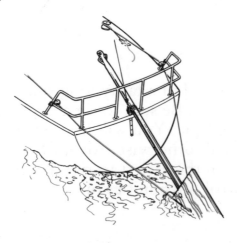

Steering with any jury rudder can be made easier by using lines led forward through blocks and around secondary cockpit winches.

153

pushpit at either outboard corner, or a spar can be lashed to the pushpit or deck and blocks can be attached to either end, in either case with lines leading from the new rudder "stock" through the blocks and thence to winches or cleats in the cockpit.

● Despite advice to the contrary, it is always better to attempt to fix the tiller at the centerline. Even without a pushpit, some makeshift arrangement can be worked out on the afterdeck, usually by lashing a spar to the mooring cleats at the quarters and affixing the rudder stock to the spar.

● A drogue can be utilized for steering—tire, bucket or proper drogue—with steering lines attached to the drogue line with rolling hitches. To give the needed steering leverage, the ends of the steering lines should be led through blocks on

In some circumstances a drogue can be used for steering, though not with the ease of a jury rudder.

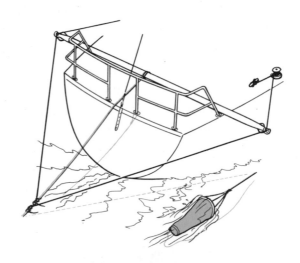

either end of a fairly long spar lashed to the stern. Be sure to rig a tripping line for the drogue. You will find recovery difficult otherwise. Also, this arrangement, though the easiest to rig, will not offer the control possibilities of a jury rudder.

Some points to consider about leaks:
- Finding a leak may be much more difficult than you might imagine. Likely spots are seacocks, rudder gland, stuffing box, keelbolts, hull-to-deck join, deck fittings—in fact anywhere the hull or deck has been drilled, cut or opened to receive a fitting. In addition, tanks . . . water, waste or fuel. Too often, the leak is far from the spot at which water collects. You may have to trace the course.
- A deck leak may be uncomfortable, but a hull leak, fitting or otherwise (skegs and keel sumps can crack from wracking strains in heavy seas) can be downright dangerous. Though the pumps may be able to cope, track it down. And don't forget the obvious: head intake hoses are usually not looped high enough. At rest this may be unnoticeable, but underway, especially when heeled, the head can overflow and cause a boat to founder. If the boat has sealed-off compartments, or if an area can be sealed off by makeshift means, do so until repairs can be effected.
- Attempt to stop the leak with rags, caulking cotton, foam or neoprene, or plugs. (Incidentally, all through-hulls, even those with seacocks, should have a tapered softwood plug of appropriate size tied to the fitting with a lanyard.) Rubber and silicon caulking will NOT hold to wet surfaces. Underwater epoxy will, and should be kept aboard for such emergencies.

Some points to consider about sail repair:
- Should the main rip along a seam, or should the stitching come undone, and the tear is below the reef points, the simplest immediate solution is reefing. If the tear is

high up, lower the sail immediately and continue to sail under foresail alone. Or hoist the storm trysail in its place until repairs can be effected. With roller reefing, there is greater latitude in just how large or small the reef can be, but after a certain point the main will lose any efficiency, driving power or ability to balance the foresail, and should be dropped and replaced.

• Should the sailcloth, not a seam, tear, best patch it on BOTH sides, either with rigging tape or, better, the special self-sticking sail-repair patches sold for the purpose. In calm conditions, patches of sailcloth and "instant" waterproof glue can effect a temporary repair. The best solution is to drop the sail, replace it with another and have the sail sent below for proper stitched repair.

• A stitched sail repair requires, in synthetic cloths, fine needles—not the canvas-piercing monsters of old—Terylene/Dacron thread and a comfortable sewing palm. Beeswax is not really necessary with modern materials. Double the thread, knot the two loose ends and close the tears with a series of herringbone stitches. With synthetic cloth, anything from 6 to 10 stitches per inch (2.5 cm), depending upon the weight of cloth, thread, etc., should be adequate.

• If the tear is larger than your four fingers minus the thumb can enter, it should be patched. A patch can be done in several different ways. Use approximately the same weight cloth as that of the sail. Or use two layers—one on either side—of lighter cloth. Seal or fold under the edges. Tape the patch in place. Fasten using a seam stitch. *Note:* Try to line up the weave

Sail patches can be bought from your sailmaker for quick temporary repairs of small tears.

of the sailcloth and the patch if possible.
With very large rips this may not be
achievable with the materials at hand. Any
patch is better than none.

● Adhesive-backed sail-repair patches are
sold for small jobs. These will usually
work for a while but are neither
permanent nor particularly suited for
heavy weather. They can be used until you
or your sailmaker makes a permanent
repair.

● Lost slides are all too common,
especially with plastic and nylon. A few
spares ought be carried, and can easily be
sewn on or, if the sail has been grommeted
along its luff, can be lashed with light
synthetic twine or tape.

● Boltropes are easily repaired with a
patch around the rope on either side,
extending several inches outward from the
rope. Sew through on both sides,
remembering to keep the patch around the
rope as tight as possible, increasing the
diameter as little as possible and thus
avoiding jams.

● If the clew fitting goes by the board, a
stout lashing will temporarily suffice.
Later on, sew in a new grommet, sew in a
rope grommet, sew in a D-ring or O-ring
replacement. In any case, make sure that
the corner of the sail is heavily reinforced
and the stitching is doubled or quadrupled.

● All sewn repairs are similar: if overlap is
possible, do it. If you can double stitch, do
it. If both sides can be patched, do it.

Taped slides are the easiest to repair and replace.

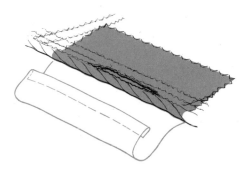

A doubled patch can repair bolt ropes that have come loose or undone.

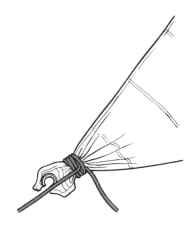

Lashing can substitute for a lost clew fitting.

157

11. Anchoring and Docking

Most sailors are used to anchoring under power with the reluctant help of their wives. A large number probably have never anchored at all, despite the hook and rode smartly displayed in the bow. This is a mistake, for not only does it keep you from the joys of peaceful anchorages, away from the peering eyes and stale air of marinas, but also it is an important safety technique in a number of circumstances.

The first question the singlehander must ask is "Where to stow the hook?" The bow is, in a small boat, the worst place—it hampers performance and is *not* convenient. The coachroof isn't bad, but not particularly

An anchor must be securely lashed, whether to the pulpit, deck fittings or a stemhead roller. The damage caused by a loose anchor is frightening to contemplate.

handy, either. I carry mine lashed either to the coachroof beside the companionway (in chocks) or lashed to the stern rail. The rode is run outside the lifelines, with about 75 feet (23 meters) clear and the rest securely cleated forward. I come into an anchorage, drop the hook from the cockpit and let her fall back. If the hook doesn't dig in, I can always go forward. But I always leave one sail up until the anchor's set, in any case.

As you might have guessed, I'm not overly fond of engines. Sure, they have their place: in calms, getting through narrow channels against the wind, maneuvering in very tight corners. Any sailor worth his salt should be able to pick up moorings and anchor or dock his vessel under sail. There may be times when you have to.

How you do any of the above under sail depends very much on your boat and its sailing characteristics. I find, especially in modern sloops and cutters, that coming in under just a small foresail, say a working jib, is best. First, you can let it fly, slowing the boat down appreciably. Second, it cannot be backed like a main, sending you scurrying off in the opposite direction. Third, you can't get smacked in the head, as with the main boom. Needless to say, at no time during any of these maneuvers should any sheets be cleated. A couple of turns on a winch and a single wrap around a cleat allows you to haul or ease at will, and both boat speed and direction will be affected by the trim of the jib.

This isn't to say you shouldn't use the engine, just that at least one driving sail must be kept set for safety's sake. Not a mizzen, and whatever it is that is hoisted—main or foresail—it should be large enough to allow maneuverability in the prevailing conditions, not too small and not too large. If no time exists for the fine points, stick to something too large. It's easier to spill wind than create it.

A roller furling or, better yet, a reefing headsail can be a godsend in singlehanded maneuvering. Since there is no such thing as

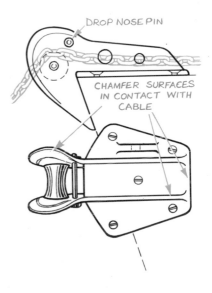

A proper stemhead chain roller.

ultimate reliability, a roller arrangement may well be the answer for you. Certainly, it is to be seriously considered if you are past the point where you enjoy dashing to the

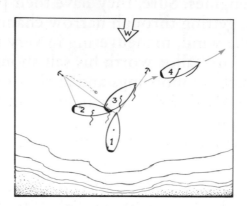

Sailing out from a two-anchor moor can be accomplished easily if you follow it step-by-step.

foredeck, lunging after runaway canvas. Be sure to keep the deck drum well lubricated. Mounted at the stemhead, it is more subject to corrosion and malfunction than anything else on the boat. And despite what manufacturers may say about "maintenance-free-performance," fresh-water rinsing and a good dollop of one of the modern Teflon or silicone lubricants can be worth its weight in gold. Bearings must not be allowed to get salty, otherwise you'll end up with an unbalanced drum with frozen bearings, and a broken gear.

In any case, whatever you choose, keep to only one sail. Handling more in any kind of weather can be truly frightening, especially when the wind is against the tide. Under those conditions, the main can back, the stern can swing around and general mayhem will ensue. Also, you avoid a tangle of sheets in the cockpit, and handling the tiller or wheel and two sets of sheets can cause anxiety out of all proportion to the task at hand.

As I mentioned previously, a staysail is both the pain and joy aboard a cutter. If it's loose-footed, it becomes the perfect

anchoring sail, provided the total area can
drive the boat in the prevailing conditions.
Too often, staysails are of an undernourished
size. This, combined with the rather aft
position of the sail, can create an unnerving
lee helm, especially on a heavy boat. But
most modern vessels are of light to moderate
displacement, which is probably better for
coastal sailing. A moderate boat with lots of
sail is far more maneuverable than the clunky
Colin Archers or pilot cutter renditions being
passed off as cruising boats.

Whatever sail you finally set, the old saw
about reaching into the anchorage usually
applies. You come in on a reach, knowing
your boat's handling characteristics, and turn
up to the spot where you'll drop your hook
or pick up the mooring—remembering that
wind and sea conditions, as well as boat speed
and displacement, will affect coasting
distances and times. Don't be dismayed if
you don't get it right initially. But allow
room to try again.

There are times when you must approach
an anchorage from downwind or to
windward. If you beat up to the hole, you
simply luff and drop. Downwind is another
matter. If your boat is highly maneuverable,
you may have enough boat speed to allow a
head-to-wind approach at the last moment. If
not, drop the hook from the stern. However,
do this with only jib up. If you try this
maneuver with the main winging out, the
chances are the boat will drag the hook or
you will beach the boat.

Do not drop the hook from the stern
when anchoring downwind unless the rode is
cleated first to the bow and then the stern.
When the boat swings head-to-wind it can
foul the rode if paid out from the bow. Once
it holds and sails are doused, you can uncleat

the stern and the boat should swing about right smartly.

Remember:

1. Ready anchor and rode on foredeck; make sure anchor is securely lashed but ready for quick release.
2. Assess anchorage for protection, windage, holding ground.
3. Double-check chart for optimum location, safety and permissibility.
4. Sail into anchorage, preferably under jib alone.
5. In your approach, try for a reach or, second best, a beat.
6. Sail to roughly the point you wish to drop the hook.
7. Turn the bows into the wind.
8. Move forward with care.
9. Unlash the anchor and let it over the side after the boat has lost forward momentum.
10. Pay out enough line for the type of holding ground and depth.
11. Snub the anchor and doubly secure the bitter end.
12. Take the bearings of your position using three structures on shore for future reference.
13. Lower and stow all sail.
14. Secure wheel or tiller.
15. Clean up boat and have a drink.

The technique for sailing into a dock or picking up a mooring isn't much different, except that you must be somewhat more aware of the boat's velocity and your ability to make it stop when you want it to. This is largely a factor of wind speed versus sail area versus sheer displacement. A heavy boat is a lot slower to respond to slacked sheets than a light flyer. You will learn this with practice, and it's well worth the effort. You can never predict when your ever-dependable diesel will conk out: usually, of course, just when you need it. Engines are particularly subject to Murphy's law.

No matter what, never let the wind get behind you approaching any solid structure, pontoon, dock, wall and so on. Invariably the structure has the advantage over the boat. Net result: one crumpled bow!

Some points to consider when anchoring:
● The state of the tide and rate of inflow and outflow are vital. In areas of small tidal range, such as the Mediterranean or

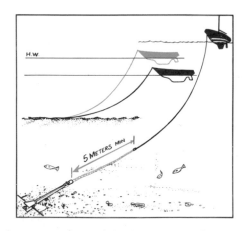

Always allow for tidal range when anchoring. With chain and rope cables, a reasonable length of chain is necessary to prevent chafe and add weight to the catenary.

the Chesapeake, this is not quite so important, but make sure you have allowed for low springs when assaying the position the boat will take when anchored. Allow for swinging room and for reversal of position when tide changes. In areas of vast tidal range, with swift inrushing tides, such as Brittany or Newfoundland, where ranges can be upward of 30 feet (9 meters), you will have to anchor far out with very long cables. In such conditions, two anchors should probably be set, especially when tides boil in at as much as 10 knots.
● Bottom composition can be determined by depth sounder, chart reference or hand

lead armed with tallow or grease. The bottom will determine the type and size of anchor you set. Mud, soft sand and mixed bottoms indicate a Danforth-type or plow anchor. Hard sand, as is found in the Aegean and Caribbean, will hold with either but may demand hand setting. Weed will foil a Danforth with ease, and sometimes a plow. Rocky bottoms will be best served with a good-old-fashioned fisherman (Herreshoff preferred—if you can find one) or a Bruce anchor. These two will usually dig past weed the best. If the bottom is mixed—small pebbles or shale, or weed and shale—use a fisherman; the goal will be to get underneath the top layer as quickly as possible. Coral accepts fishermen and plows best, though the shank of a plow can be badly bent by coral and chain cable is almost a necessity to avoid chafe. If it can be found, I have discovered the Northill anchor to be the most effective over the widest range of conditions.

● Too often anchors are tossed, dropped or slung over the bows. By carefully and slowly lowering it you will be able to ascertain the rate of drift, and will avoid permanently damaging the hull, deck or yourself.

● Scope depends upon depth at high water, holding ground and whether chain or rope cable. All rope cables should have at least 15 feet (4.5 meters) of chain between the end of the rope and the anchor to prevent chafe and increase holding power. All chain permits shorter scope (as little as 3:1), but can snub more easily than rope. Rope, having great elasticity (nylon), will act as a better shock absorber, especially when in surging conditions. However, rope must be heavily padded—with either patent chafe gear or rags or leather—to avoid catastrophe at the stemhead, roller or chocks. The holding ground will make a difference; the better the bottom, the less the scope. Mud and soft sand will usually hold best, assuming the appropriate anchor. In any case, be prepared to set rope cable with a minimum of 6:1 scope and chain with a minimum of 4:1 scope. With deteriorating weather and sea conditions, scope should be increased and the possibility of setting a second or even third anchor must be considered.

• Making sure the anchor is set is the most important single step you can take in anchoring. Either back the sails, throw the engine in reverse or hand snub it when the appropriate amount of scope has been paid out. Be sure the cable is attached to a strong point below decks and is secured to the samson post, cleat or anchor winch. Even with chain cable a nylon preventer is a good idea—especially as cables have an appalling tendency to snap at the stemhead fitting or roller—rigged from a second cleat inboard to the cable a couple of feet or meters outboard of the stem. Not only can this save you an anchor and cable but also will act as a shock absorber in heavy surge situations.

• Not only should the inboard end of the cable be securely fastened to the ship but also the cable must be bowsed down in the proper stemhead fitting. In a roller, the cheeks must be high enough to prevent the cable from jumping out; a retaining pin should be fitted, and all metal should be filed down so that no sharp edges are evident at any point at which the cable

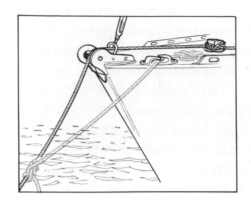

One possible method of securing the cable as well as taking strain off the cable is shown here. Deck cleats must be very strong to allow this maneuver.

might touch the roller or cheeks. Chain can be weakened by friction against metal! If your roller lacks a retaining pin, or if you must pass the cable through a chock, use a short length of light stuff to tie down the rope or chain, either around the fitting or in some way to close off the opening.

● When the wind shows signs of veering, be prepared to lay out a second anchor. The second anchor can be the kedge and can be equipped with chain and rope cable.

Setting out a second anchor will bring peace of mind in any situation when the wind shows signs of veering.

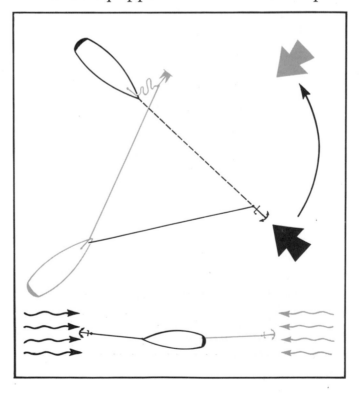

Lower it off the bows in the direction
from which the wind is veering. Pay out
cable as the boat begins to swing until
more or less equal strain is taken by both
anchors.

● In a river or where the tidal stream runs
strong and will reverse, or where there is
little or no room to swing, anchoring fore-
and-aft is called for. Anchor in the normal
way, letting out double the amount of
cable needed for the situation—a good
reason to carry at least 250 to 280 feet (75
to 100 meters) of cable—and set the hook.
Then drop a stern anchor and motor or
winch the ship forward, paying out an
amount of cable to get the ship midway
between the 2 anchors. Be sure to station
someone in the bow to take in the excess
cable at the same time you are moving
forward, otherwise you chance fouling the
propeller or wrapping a rope cable around
the keel or skeg or rudder. Be sure to
allow a small amount of slack—at high
water—in both cables, but not so much as
to make for uncomfortable movement.

● Anchoring in heavy weather or off a lee
shore is always a fearful and difficult
experience. However, there are times when
no other alternative permits itself. Two
basic methods are available for effective
holding power. *First:* Drop one anchor in
the normal manner, paying out double the
length of cable needed. Lay a second—
much as in the fore-and-aft technique—
bringing up on the first cable. If the two
anchors are laid one to windward and one
to leeward, the chances of holding in a
wind shift are greatly increased—especially
important if anchoring not far offshore in
an open roadstead. Lay out extra cable so
that both lines will not foul the underbody

of the boat. *Second:* Use two anchors in line. That is, attach the kedge with a length of chain to the bower ring with a shackle. Lower the kedge first, then the bower, while making sternway. Or, drop the bower first, with the kedge attached aft on the cable at a distance at least equal to the depth of the water, certainly no less than 25 feet (7.5 meters). Remember, in any storm situation the strains on deck attachment points will be excessive. Make sure that chain cable can be released instantly if you must drop the anchor and run. Buoy the chain before releasing it.

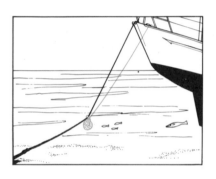

A weight or sack of weights let down the anchor cable on a messenger line allows you to shorten scope in overcrowded anchorages.

• Dragging can be much more than a nuisance. On a lee shore it can be deadly. If your boat begins to drag—something you can tell from reference to landmarks—start the engine first! Then pay out more cable. If this does not work, motor up, taking in cable, and reset the anchor. If the bottom is suspect, try running a riding weight down the anchor cable. This can be a patent device or a ball of chain. Just make sure that whatever weight you use is reasonably heavy, say equal to the weight of the kedge anchor. If this does not work effectively, set a second anchor at an angle of 25 to 35 degrees.

• There are times when you will foul the anchor, either on seabed refuse or underwater cables or with another anchor. First, try hauling in cable until it is vertical and taut. Then move weight aft to try breaking it out or supply appropriate leverage via a windlass. If this doesn't work, try sailing or motoring out, pulling in the opposite direction from which the anchor was originally set. So much for the easy methods. All the rest take a certain amount of real and imaginary labor. You can run a loop of line or chain down over the anchor cable, carry it out in the dinghy and then haul from the opposite direction. Or you can use a grapnel (or a small hook as such) from the *anchored* dinghy to try to pick up the main anchor, or any

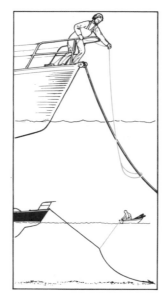

Messengers can be used to clear a fouled anchor or tangled cables.

obstructing cable. If the anchor and cable are fouled by another boat's ground tackle, attempt to raise both anchor *and* cable, securing it by a line to the boat as you lift the pair higher and higher. Then try to free the anchor by hand from the dinghy (tethered to the mother ship).

• When the chance exists that you will be in a crowded anchorage (what isn't, these days?) or expect that you shall have to depart an anchorage with greater dispatch than you had perhaps originally planned, it is a good idea to set up a buoyed trip line. Very simply, attach a length of reasonably light cordage (⅜ inch or 8 mm) to the crown of the anchor before lowering it. To the "top" end, tie a short length of chain to steady it and a small buoy or plastic bottle. This will tend to keep other boats

A trip line, buoyed at the surface, can be a godsend when confronted with a fouled anchor.

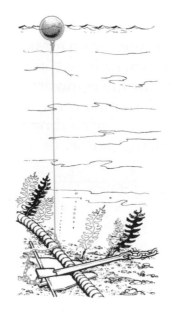

away; should the anchor become fouled, will give you a ready-set method for breaking it free.

● At first, setting an anchor single handed can be a frantic experience. Remember to lower and secure the mainsail. You will find it much easier to handle the boat under just foresail and without the danger of swinging booms and backing sails. Pass the rode or cable outside of all stanchions and lines aft to the cockpit, making sure the cable is secured, with the necessary scope, to the foredeck. You can release both anchor and jib sheets together, calmly move forward and snub anchor and lower the jib one after the other. Release latches

Singlehanders would be well advised to consider this arrangement for anchoring from the cockpit. Make sure all lines are led outside the lifelines.

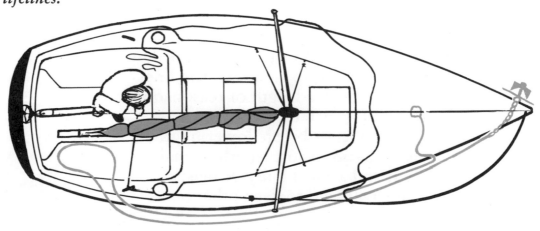

to drop the anchor from a roller chock are not to be recommended. They have a tendency to stick or you may release the anchor and accidentally overshoot the rode, creating a large tangled mass about the underwater appendages of your boat.

Some points to consider when docking:
• Approaching any dock or quay or pontoon is made more difficult by the tight quarters, proximity of other vessels and the tricks tidal streams can play amongst pilings and walls. Make due allowance for windage, drift and lost control at low speeds. Know how your

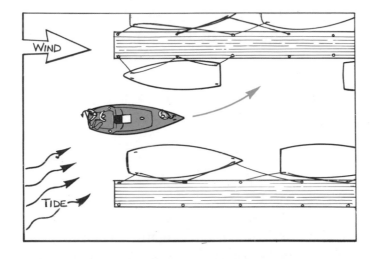

Approaching a dock or quay, precautions must be made to keep the boat moving only fast enough to allow maneuverability. Prepare to stop the boat, either through lines to the pilings or by engine, as soon as possible.

ship handles! Attempt to approach to windward. With wind and tide behind you, you will have to either play with bursts of reverse on the throttle or have a crew member stationed to drop a stern anchor to slow down the ship and allow for some control. The same maneuver can be practiced with current abeam.
• Cleat all lines and pass through chocks, then outboard and over any rails or lifelines. Secure all fenders overboard. If approaching a concrete or stone pier, use

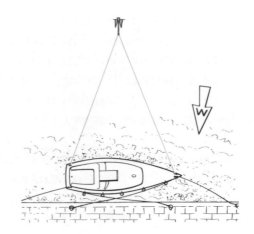

fenderboards. Quite often the pier will be quite high; be prepared to scale the wall (hope there is a ladder) with both bow *and* stern lines in hand. Spring lines can be rigged after bow and stern are secured. Should the ship be tied up on the windward side of the dock, a kedge can be run out to hold it off, either from a spring cleat amidships or with two warps leading from the kedge to both bow and stern cleats.

● You may suddenly have to change your intended approach or goal because of either the unexpected appearance of a smaller, hitherto unseen, boat or directions from the dockmaster. Lines, fenders, etc. will have to be quickly switched. If you have enough time, it pays to back off and reapproach *after* these chores have been completed. If not, and the area is crowded on first approach, it is a good idea to rig lines and fenders on both sides of the yacht. In places like St. Peter Port or Newport or Annapolis, at the height of the season, docking is always at a premium. Plan accordingly.

● In most of the Mediterranean, tying up stern-to is the norm. This is accomplished by letting out the best bower about 100 feet (30 meters) plus the length of the ship from the quay and backing toward the dock. Unfortunately, with adverse conditions this can be at best a tricky maneuver. Better to drop the hook from the stern and go in bow first. Most boats have greater control in forward, as well as greater stopping power. In addition, should you desire such things, your

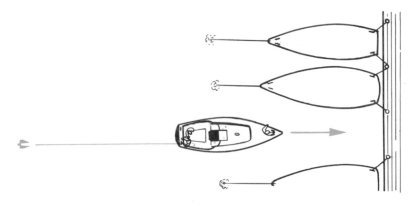

Mediterranean moors are usually stern-to. Try entering bow on, as this will give you much greater control over the yacht, especially when alone.

privacy will be that much more. If you wish you can end-for-end the bow and anchor lines—providing there is room port and starboard—and turn the ship around. If boats are wedged in on both sides, extend the line to the quay and haul well clear of your neighbors before attempting to make the turn.

• Should the berth be one that dries out at low tide, attempt to heel the boat slightly inward toward the quay. A line passed about the mast at spreader height and led ashore will usually do the trick. Be careful that the rigging does not come in contact with the dock, and that the spreaders will not be damaged. A block attached to a halyard and also held around the mast with a strop or loose loop of rope can be hoisted aloft to just below the spreaders *after* a line from the dock has been led

A line ashore, when moored to a quay, will make for good insurance in an area where the yacht may dry out at low tide.

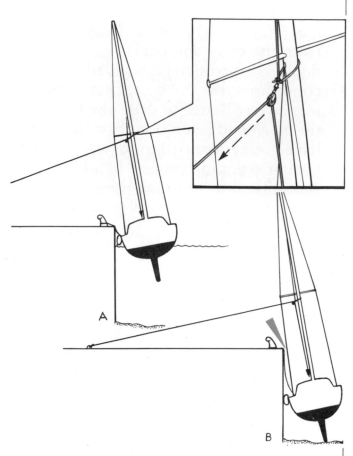

Endless-loop mooring lines allow a singlehander to cast off from the helm without dockside assistance.

through it and back to the dock or to a cleat on deck. In addition, a heavy anchor can be placed on the dockside deck of the vessel.

● Be sure in any tidal area that enough slack is kept in the docking line to allow for the rise and fall of the ship. A good idea is to lead the lines to the dock pilings or cleats in a bight and then back again to the deck cleats. In this manner, you will be able to make adjustments without leaving the deck.

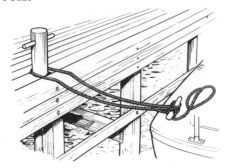

12. Dinghies

Hard or inflatable, towed or hoisted aboard, a dinghy is your lifeline to shore. And, if you don't have a life raft aboard, it is your major buoyancy aid as well.

If your boat is under 35 feet (10.5 meters), you will not be able to carry a solid dink unless the foredeck is flush or the space between companionway and mast is long and clear (no lines back to the cockpit here!). Your options include davits or towing. Davits are dangerous for two reasons—they are vulnerable to following seas and they add considerable weight aft. In the days of heavy displacement, this was fine, but a few hundred pounds or kilos hanging from the afterdeck of a lighter boat will have an appreciable effect on performance. Also, both davits and deck stowage add an enormous amount of windage, and will probably hamper your progress to windward.

Towing is fine, killing only a knot or less from boat speed. However, the strains on the deck gear, towline and bow fittings of the dink are enormous. Also, someone has to keep an eye on the dink. Weaving back and forth, surging, flipped or driven into the stern of the mother ship, a towed dink is a poor traveling companion, in my opinion. Others will disagree, but when alone, you have enough to worry about without adding the bother of a trailing albatross.

Having gone through all the possibilities, I have come to settle on a good inflatable— Zodiac, Avon, Achilles, Beaufort, Dunlop, etc.—for ease of stowage, stability (important, when alone, to a greater degree than you might imagine) and convenience. Sure, they don't row like a peapod or a good skiff, but they don't create any problems when you are *not* using them. They demand absolutely no attention when you're under sail.

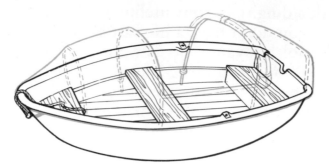

A dinghy can be turned into a liferaft with foresight and some work. Flotation, a canopy, stores and some means of propulsion must be added.

I don't like small motors. They are inconvenient to stow and mount, leak gas and generally get in the way. If you feel too decrepit to handle oars, then get one by all means. If you wish to use oars, buy ones with leathers and solid oarlocks, made preferably of spruce. Ash oars are the norm—and they are twice the weight of spruce. That makes quite a difference on a long haul to shore.

Inflatables give you less choice, and the strokes used must be modified—short and strong rather than the long and easy strokes used rowing a boat. Make sure you always carry a bailer and a small anchor (well protected in blow-up boats—the folding Norwegian type is good) with rode. You may come across an unknown current and not be able to fight it, even with a motor. Floorboards are necessary for inflatables, and handholds for rowboats. Thwarts must be adjustable and foot braces are lovely if you can fit them.

Your inflatable should be clearly identified and easy to handle alone. A 300-pound (135 kg) rowing skiff has no place in a singlehander's inventory.

Some points to consider about your dinghy:

- More deaths are probably caused by swamped and capsized dinghies than by anything else on the water. The average tender is perhaps 8 or 10 feet (2.5 or 3 meters) in length and cannot really hold more than three people in anything but a dead calm. In truly rough water, no more than two should attempt a journey. As well as not overloading with people, you must be careful to avoid masses of gear, especially in the ends of the boat. Try to keep the boat trimmed and balanced, both athwartships and fore-and-aft.

When boarding a dinghy from a dock or quay, always step into the center of the boat while holding onto the edge of the dock or a rail. Sit down squarely as soon as possible. Only then should you consider untying the painter.

- The novice will inevitably step on the gunwale when trying to board. This can lead to lacerations or a dunking. In most hard tenders, you can step directly into the center portion of the floorboards. However, if the dock or float is particularly high, you may have to alight on the center thwart and descend quickly. The idea is to sit down as quickly as possible. NEVER board a dinghy with your hands full. Either load first or enter and then transfer the cargo once you are seated.

● Most dinghy oars are far too short, too heavy, and ill balanced. Ideally, they should fit into the tender, be made of spruce and shaped to be comfortable to use, and be efficient at propelling the boat. Far too few people ever bother to learn to row properly. The beamier the boat, the shorter the strokes; also, the heavier the seas, the shorter the strokes is a fairly sound rule of thumb. However, load, windage, sea state, wetted surface all play a part in the best (read: most effective, least tiring) way to row. Practice. And be sure that you have oarlocks, leathers and a rowing position—with foot brace—that can stand up to the job. Trial and error will find the way.

● Getting the dink into the water and back on board is the first concern of the cruising sailor. It must always be tethered to the mother ship. Too often a perfect launch is followed by a perfect drift into the distance. Obviously, the method of launching is dependent upon the ship, but usually some sort of hoist and tackle arrangement will be necessary to accomplish the job with minimum fuss and danger.

One means of launching a hard dinghy from the deck, using the boom as a hoist. A sling arrangement can easily be made, as shown here.

• Probably the greatest danger—other than overloading—is in landing or launching through surf. This is NEVER a deed to be undertaken lightly! With oar power, the difficulty will be to restrain the dinghy enough or propel it fast enough. With an outboard, the problems are stalling, cavitation and general unreliability if swamped. And that is the danger: swamping, or capsize. If the surf is running with any power, you would be well advised to stay on the ship or on the beach. Otherwise, you'll need a large enough boat to power through. Do not underestimate the power of breaking seas.

13. Self-Steering

The most exhausting part of singlehanded sailing is sitting at the wheel or tiller for hours on end. Even if you intend to keep to coastal hops, self-steering is something you must seriously consider for passages of more than 35 miles (56 km). Yet very few boats have been equipped with self-steering devices, at least in the United States. They are far more common in England and France.

Remember, however, self-steering does not take the place of a proper lookout. It cannot avoid obstacles. It will aid in avoiding fatigue, however, and permit you to navigate coastal passages with greater comfort and safety. It must be used with discretion and never in congested or crowded areas—

moorings, harbor entrances, channels and shipping lanes.

Self-steering devices fall into two broad categories: wind powered and electrically driven. Under the first heading come all wind vanes and sheet-to-tiller rigs, no matter what degree of complexity or simplicity they may maintain. Under the second come all autopilots. The important thing to keep in mind when choosing a system is that wind vanes keep course to the tune of the apparent wind, while autopilots follow a compass course, no matter what.

The advantages of one over the other are dependent on the average wind strength in your usual cruising grounds, the time you'll be under power and the design and balance of your boat. An autopilot can be used with sails alone only if the wind is steady and from one quadrant. Otherwise, you will spend most of your time trimming sails, and your fatigue factor will go up. Just what you're trying to avoid.

Yet, in light wind areas, a wind vane, unless very friction-free and reasonably sophisticated (servo-pendulum), will not be able to transfer the wind strength into enough force to steer the boat effectively. Donald Hamilton, the author of the Matt Helm books, uses an autopilot on his 27-foot (8 meters) cutter and is very satisfied with its performance. But he also does much of his singlehanding in light air, at night and under power.

Many sailors feel they must be at the tiller when the wind pipes up. After all, isn't that the rationale for sailing? For daysailing, and with a crew, yes. But when you are alone, energy conservation is of prime importance, and you can be equally thrilled standing in the bows while the wind vane fights the tiller on its own.

Vanes usually work best when beating, since most boats can be made to balance themselves and sail a reasonably true course to windward. In any case, a vane will enhance the accuracy of the course steered. The vane will, in fact, steer a better course than you, since it is more sensitive to changes, gusts and such. Also, it is always working and will automatically correct all the errors a helmsman might make once his powers of concentration have begun to diminish. Over a long period of time, the vane will outperform Ted Turner or Paul Elvstrom.

Since the apparent wind is much less downwind, a vane will tend to be more erratic on this point of sailing. It is constantly responding to slight wind changes. Thus, downwind, where the boat's directional stability is lessened, the vane will steer from one side to the other. The true course will probably average out, but to an observer ashore, it may well look as if a slightly tipsy sailor has taken the helm.

On a reach, the gear will respond in relation to the wind speed. Heavy air will cause—again, with exceptions—more erratic behavior than moderate air. And too much sail up can cause wild gyrations. In other words, the sail power can overcome any mechanical advantage the vane would normally have.

If you sail a small boat without engine, as I do, there's really no choice. But deciding on which vane to buy is another matter. Much depends on the shape of the hull, the sail plan and the natural directional stability of the boat. Generally, long, slim hulls with the rudder aft-mounted on a substantial skeg will have greater directional stability than a fat IOR-styled underbody. Spade rudders, which have little or no place on an offshore boat, are

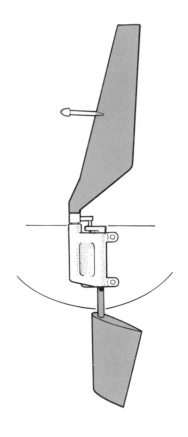

All wind vanes work on a similar principle. The vane activates the rudder or an auxiliary rudder or a trim tab attached to the main rudder. The pressure applied causes the rudder to move and turn the yacht. Countless variations exist, with different mechanisms, gearing and configurations. You should discuss the matter with a expert before installing one, because each and every hull has specific characteristics that must be taken into account before fitting any gear.

variable in their response to the helm. Those on Ted Hood's and Bill Lapworth's boats are slightly balanced and have a vertical stock. They seem to be more responsive. The new breed of boats designed by Holland, Peterson and Frers have enormous rudders but are designed for massive power, which is not needed for self-steering.

Long keels will usually supply a steady helm but make the boat less maneuverable. Compromise is creeping up on us. Moderation is again the keynote. A moderate boat with moderate overhangs, reasonable draft to prevent leeway and a large rudder seems to be the best all-round solution. This assumes you'll use the boat for daysailing, coastal hops, occasional races and offshore passages. No boat is ideal, but the more traditional boat will do more of these tasks better. By traditional I don't mean some bogged-down, turn-of-the-century pilot boat, but something more like the CCA or RORC boats of the 1960s and early 1970s.

In any case, the moderate boat will demand less of a self-steering vane than some out-and-out racing machine. Less demand means less expense. Small cruisers with decent lateral plane can get by on a vane-to-tiller setup. Whether the vane is pivoted

Some sort of release mechanism for wind-vane steering gear is a necessity for the singlehander. A snap shackle spliced into the tiller control lines with a trailing line led overboard may be the only way to stop the yacht should you fall overboard. Little thought of, this is a matter for serious consideration; some means of releasing the self-steering must be devised. This is, of course, an even greater problem with autopilots; some sort of self-tripping relay may be possible.

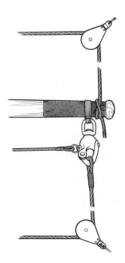

vertically or horizontally is a matter of choice, though the horizontal vane will generally exert greater power. With this system, bearings and pivots must be as friction-free as possible, and the tiller lines as taut as possible. The newer nonstretch Dacron for halyards works well. Assuming there is no mizzen to contend with, the vane is best mounted as high and as far aft as possible.

If you happen to have a transom-hung rudder and you wish a greater range of self-steering abilities, a trim-tab system may be the answer. Developed by "Blondie" Hasler, the OSTAR originator, this form of vane apparatus works by having the vane actuate a small trim tab attached to the trailing edge of the rudder. When the vane is turned by a change in wind direction, through a linkage system it turns the trim tab, which in turn causes the rudder to swing and correct course.

Beyond these, vanes quickly become more expensive and more complicated, and if your boat is in the 35-foot-and-over (10.5 meters) range you will have to opt for one of these more sophisticated systems. The vane-to-tiller set-up hasn't the power, and you won't find many transom-hung rudders on larger boats.

The answer in such cases is a pendulum vane gear. Here the trim tab is actually an independent pendulum in the water and turns on both horizontal and vertical axes. Thus it will be forced by the pressure of the water to assume the same position as the centerline of the boat and will turn vertically at the same time to actuate the helm via tiller lines.

Variations exist, some with their own auxiliary rudders, some with adjustable linkages, some with horizontal or vertical vanes, some with smaller vanes, and so on. The principles are all the same, and in choosing a vane gear you must take into account the boat's performance as well as its general handling characteristics. Gerard Dijkstra's excellent little book *Self-Steering for Sailboats* is the best general guide to the subject, though John Letcher's *Self-Steering for Sailing Craft* is more complete but also more technical.

You will have to experiment to some degree. I know of only two vane gear manufacturers who essentially custom-build vanes for particular boats. Otherwise, you buy off the shelf.

Remember, your choice must be dictated by the sailing characteristics, hull type and sail plan of your ship. If you have money to burn, units like the Mustafa or Sailomat will steer almost anything, but their cost is very high. Some of the smaller vanes, especially the French Navik, are reasonable in cost, light and reliable. If you have a wheel, you will have to make or buy a drum attachment to allow the tiller lines to work (or get an auxiliary rudder set-up).

A final possibility is sheet-to-tiller rigs. A great deal of trial-and-error experimentation is necessary, however, to get them to work.

Appendix A:

Spares and Tools

Boats From 30 to 45 Feet (9 to 14 Meters)

Tools
8″ (20 cm) adjustable wrench
medium size pliers
medium blade screwdriver
10″ (25 cm) vise grips
pocket rigging knife with spike
Dacron pouch or waterproof bag to carry tools

Sail repair kit

scissors
sailmaker's wax
palm
seam ripper
hot knife
3 spools waxed polyester
needles (5 each #'s 15 & 17)
1 roll Rip-stop tape
3′×3′ (1×1 meter) piece of adhesive sticky-back Dacron
light thread for spinnaker repair, telltale yarn
nylon dittybag to contain all the above

Spare parts

assorted stainless steel nuts, bolts, washers, sheet metal screws
bulbs for compass and running lights
winch pawls and springs
cam cleat springs
cotter pins (stainless steel, 2 of each size used) and split rings
small clear plastic tackle box to contain above

Odds and ends

1 roll of silver duct tape (Nashua 357)
tube of clear silicone seal
1 can WD-40
small can 3-in-1 oil
Magic Marker (black)
can of (Moly Coat) Never-Seize
nylon dittybag to hold the above

Boats From 30 to 45 Feet (9 to 14 Meters)

Tools
Allen wrenches
chisels (1 cold)
drills (hand drill plus set of bits)
files (8″ or 20 cm mill bastard, 1 medium size rattail, 1 triangular)
hammer (medium ball-peen)
50′ (15 meters) measuring tape
nail set
oil stone
pliers (channel locks, needle nose, 2 regular)
saw (hacksaw plus at least 10 high-speed blades)
screwdrivers (6 assorted sizes regular, 2 Phillips head, 1 jeweler's set)
vise grips (7″ and 10″ or 18 and 25 cm)
wire brush
wire cutters (medium size Felco's)
work gloves
wrenches (8″ and 10″ or 20 and 25 cm adjustable, set of combination—open end and box)
wooden tool box or dry organized area to store all the above

Electrical parts

spare bulb for each light aboard
3 each spare fuses for each kind aboard
assorted wire crimps
wire stripper/crimpers
flashlight batteries and bulbs
continuity tester
black electrical tape

Engine and mechanical spares

3 cans of oil for hydraulics
hydraulic hose and assorted end fittings
transmission fluid
set of engine filters
assorted grits wet/dry sandpaper
complete set engine belts
enough oil for oil change

new voltage regulator for each alternator
6'×6' (2×2 meters) canvas drop cloth with
     grommets
piece of plywood
piece of wood (2×4)
assorted hose clamps
drift punch

Spares

assorted nuts, bolts and washers
5 of each size cotter key used aboard
assorted clevis pins
assorted "D" shackles
assorted snap shackles
1 standing rigging toggle
1 genoa car
winch pawls
winch pawl springs
winch roller bearings

Sail repair kit

scissors
sailmaker's wax
2 palms
2 seam rippers
hot knife
light thread for spinnaker repairs
6 spools waxed polyester
needles (10 each #'s 13, 15, 17, 19)
Rip-stop tape
3'×6' (1×2 meters) piece of sticky-back
     Dacron
yarn for telltales
25' (5.75 meters) seizing wire
3 "D" rings
sailmaker's pliers
nylon bag to hold all the above

Sealers and lubricants

2-part epoxy
2 tubes clear silicone seal
2 cans WD-40
can CRC 666
can 3-in-1 oil
silicone spray
special grease mixture
rolls of colored tape

2 rolls of duct tape
Magic Markers (black)
1 can Felpro C5A

Yachts 45 Feet (14 Meters) and Larger

Tools

Allen wrenches (long and short)
awls (small and large)
block plane
chisels (1 cold, 2 regular)
drills (brace, hand drill, 3/8" or 1 cm chuck
     variable-speed reversible electric drill, 2
     sets of metal bits)
files (8", 10", 12" or 20, 25, 30 cm mill
     bastards, 3 wood files, 2 rattails, 1
     triangular)
hammers (16 oz. or 500 grams ball-peen, baby
     sledge, claw and rubber mallet)
measures (100' or 30 meters measuring tape,
     fold-up ruler, calipers)
mirror (1 retrieving)
nail sets (5 assorted)
oil stone
pipe cutter
pipe length (for battering ram)
pliers (2 channel locks, 2 needle nose, 4
     regular in assorted sizes)
putty knives (two 1" or 2.5 cm)
saws (crosscut, hacksaw and 40 blades, jigsaw
     and 12 blades)
screwdrivers (17 assorted regular, 6 assorted
     Phillips head, 2 offset, 1 jeweler's set)
tape and die set (including 8–32, 10–24,
     10–32, 1/4–20, 5/16–24, 3/8–16, 3/8–24)
tin snips
torch set propare
vise
vise grips (7" and 10" or 18 and 25 cm)
wire brushes
wire cutters
work gloves
wrenches (6", 8", 10" or 15, 20, 25 cm
     adjustables; 14" or 36 cm pipe wrench,
     strap wrench, complete 3/8" or 1 cm drive
     socket set, complete set combination
     wrenches, popular sizes of open-end
     wrenches)

X-Acto knife and 6 blades
wooden tool box to contain the above

Electrical parts

compass-light assembly
running-light bulbs
spare bulb for each brand of lamp aboard
3 of each kind of fuse aboard
assorted wire crimps
wire stripper-crimpers
flashlight batteries and bulbs
assorted sizes of wire
black electrical tape
silicone grease
multimeter
solder
soldering gun or iron
spare anemometer cups
spare wind vane
spare knotmeter transducers
tackle box for the above

Sealers and lubricants

2 part epoxy
2 tubes clear silicone sealer
2 cans WD-40
2 cans CRC 666
2 non-aerosol cans 3-in-1 oil
2 cans silicone spray
special grease mixture
1 can Felpro C5A
2 rolls duct tape
2 rolls of each colored tape
2 Magic Markers (black)
Dacron bag to hold the above

Sail repair kit

scissors
sailmaker's wax
2 palms
2 seam rippers
hot knife and spare tip
light thread for spinnaker repairs
8 spools waxed polyester
needles (1 package each of #'s 13, 15, 17, 19)
2 rolls Rip-stop spinnaker repair tape
two 3'×6' (1×2 meters) pieces sticky-backed
    Dacron

yarn (red, green and blue for telltales)
2 weights seizing wire (25' or 5.75 meters
    each)
3 "D" or "O" rings
50' (15 meters) tubular webbing
sailmaker's pliers
assorted weight sailcloth
roll 5 oz. Dacron tape, 6" width
spool ⁵⁄₃₂" flag halyard
6 awls
grommet set (stud, spur, mallet, die, rings,
    liners)
Dacron bag to hold the above

Rigging parts

Nico-press tool (size of halyards, 2
    preferable)
12 Nico-press sleeves for each size wire
    aboard
assorted stainless steel thimbles
assorted snap shackles
assorted "D" shackles
several lengths different weights of wire (15"
    each)
assorted rigging toggles
assorted clevis pins
assorted track cars
link plate set
spare main halyard
spare genoa halyard
good-sized turnbuckle
plastic fishing-tackle box for above

Engine and mechancial spares

gallon of oil for hydraulic rigging adjusters
10' (2.5 meters) length hydraulic hose,
    assorted fittings
2 cans transmission fluid
oil for engine oil change
set engine filters, gaskets
complete set engine belts
voltage regulator for each alternator
6'×6' (2×2 meters) canvas drop cloth with
    grommets
assorted hose clamps
piece of plywood
2 pieces 3' (1 meters) long 2×4s
drift punch
set of injectors

grease gun with special grease
2 cans starting spray (Ether)
keel-bolt wrench
rudder-packing wrench
spare set steering cables
master links (12) for steering chain and
    spinnaker pole chain

Spares

clear plastic tackle box containing 12 of each
    size SS cotter pins
clear plastic box of nuts, bolts, washers (12
    each size including #'s 6, 8, 12 and ¼",
    5⁄16", 3⁄8")
head repair kit: spare pump parts,
    diaphragms, impellers
hand pump for bilge, for changing oil
electric drill pump, hoses
1 sleeve bronze wool
12 sheets each wet/dry sandpaper in 220, 400,
    600 grits
three sheets each crocus cloth, emery paper
spare packing for propeller and rudder glands

Winch parts

12 pawls
24 pawl springs
assorted roller bearings
6 split rings
tooth brush
tweezers
dental pick
extra handle
clear plastic box to hold the above

Optional

banding tool, bands, and clips

Appendix B:

Suggested First Aid Kit

Injectables

Decadron solution, 4 mg per ml*
Adrenalin (epinephrine 1 to 1000)*
Demerol, 4 mg per ml*
sterile 2-ml syringes with 23-gauge needles*
sterile 1-ml syringes with 25-gauge needles*

Injuries

assorted sizes of Band-Aids
sterile packages of 2"×2" and 4"×4" sterile
    gauze pads
adhesive tape
sterile roller gauze of self-clinging type
cotton balls
sterile Swats
box of assorted finger splints
wrist splints, right-handed and left-handed
Betadine solution
package of Steri-Strips
package of sterile petroleum jelly gauze
suture set, packaged and sterile. Needle
    holder, thumb forceps, scissors
sterile packages of #4-0 silk suture material
    on swedged-on needles
1% Xylocaine local anesthetic solution*

Seasickness

Dramamine
Marezine
Triptone
Bucladin*

Pain (oral medications)

aspirin, 5-grain tablets or capsules
acetaminophen (Tylenol, Datril, Phenaphen,
    Tempra), 5-grain tablets or capsules
Empirin Compound with Codeine #3*
Acetaminophen with Codeine #3*
Pyridium, 100-mg tablets*
* Needs doctor's prescription.

Infection

Erythromycin, 400-mg* or capsules
Gantrisin, 500-mg tablets*
Ampicillin, 500-mg tablets*
Tetracycline, 250-mg* or capsules
Nafcillin, 500-mg tablets*
Chloroquine tablets (for malaria only)*

Allergies

Chlor-Trimeton, 4-mg tablets

Digestive disorders

Lomotil tablets (syrup for children)*
Colace tablets (syrup for children)
Fleet enema (pediatric strength for children)
glycerin suppositories
Pepto-Bismol
Tigan, 200-mg suppositories*

Respiratory disorders

cough medicine—any mild nonprescription
    medication
Phenergan Expectorant with Codeine*
nose drops or nasal spray—any brand
antihistamine/decongestant ("cold
    remedy")—any brand that does not
    contain aspirin

Poisoning

syrup of ipecac

Sedation

Valium, 5-mg tablets*

Local applications (eyes, ears, skin)

Visine eye drops
10% Sulamyd ophthalmic solution*
Cortisporin ear solution*
Sun filter cream with para-aminobenzoic acid
    (PABA) or other without PABA for the
    allergic
Petroleum jelly
Desenex ointment and powder
Neosporin ointment
rubbing alcohol
Hydrocortisone cream or lotion
Lotrimin cream*

Miscellaneous equipment

Oxygen tank and mask
Snake bite kit for expeditions ashore and
    poisonous fish vites

* Needs doctor's prescription.

Index